FLOWERING HOUSE PLANTS

MONTH BY MONTH

Other Books by Jack Kramer

Growing Orchids at Your Windows   1963
Bromeliads, The Colorful House Plants   1965

FLOWERING
HOUSE PLANTS
MONTH BY MONTH

By JACK KRAMER

Drawings by Andrew R. Addkison

 VAN NOSTRAND REINHOLD COMPANY
NEW YORK   CINCINNATI   TORONTO   LONDON   MELBOURNE

VAN NOSTRAND REINHOLD COMPANY REGIONAL OFFICES:
New York   Cincinnati   Chicago   Millbrae   Dallas

VAN NOSTRAND REINHOLD COMPANY INTERNATIONAL OFFICES:
London   Toronto   Melbourne

Acknowledgment for the color photographs (following pages 34 and
82) is made as follows: Figures 4, 5, 7, 8, 9, A. R. Addkison; 1, 2, 6,
Joyce R. Wilson; 3, Brown Bulb Ranch.

Published by VAN NOSTRAND REINHOLD COMPANY
450 West 33rd Street, New York, N.Y. 10001

Published simultaneously in Canada by
VAN NOSTRAND REINHOLD LIMITED

About
Flowering House Plants

Some ten years ago, I made a search for flowering plants that would grow at home. I hunted in florists' shops and greenhouses throughout the city and suburbs, and after many weeks all I had to show for my work was a small Clivia and a Crown-of-Thorns. I found foliage plants in many sizes, leaf colors, and shapes, but the *flowering* indoor plant was as scarce as the legendary Black Orchid. In this hunt, I became interested in Orchids. Although these could not be found locally either, the growers were more interested in talking about them, and soon I discovered many mail-order houses. Hence my books *Growing Orchids at Your Windows*, and, later, *Bromeliads, The Colorful House Plants*.

In my travels through the years visiting orchid ranges from New York to Miami to Seattle, I began to find the flowering plants I had originally looked for. Although growing Orchids and Bromeliads pretty well filled my spare time, I could not resist occasionally buying a few pots of other flowering plants.

When the east sun-room of my apartment became available two years ago I decided to use it as a growing area for flowering subjects. (The Orchids and Bromeliads grow in the west plant room.) Some of the flowering species I grow are "new" plants—that is, they have been imported only recently; others are old favorites that have been forgotten. As far as possible, in this book I have concentrated on the more unusual kinds. Florists are beginning to stock a few flowering house plants, and many mail-order houses now offer a wide selection of species and varieties.

So more than ten years have passed and I continue my original quest, but with more satisfaction. I now grow many flowering plants. Of these, some are more dependable than others, some better for home decoration than others, and many produce an exceptionally colorful display. There are those that have not responded to my efforts, and I will speak of them too. I now have 300 plants that thrive under average house conditions in my city apartment. I may regulate temperature somewhat or increase the humidity, but all this is little effort in return for the thrill of seeing colorful flowers at the windows. There are thousands of species to choose from and among those that flower are many inexpensive beauties.

It is customary in many gardening books to give culture first. However, because the emphasis in this book is on selection of plants for bloom, information on growing follows the description of each of the multitude of plants that will bring color to your windows all through the year. In Part II will be found a general cultural discussion as well as a list of plants to buy for a start and recommended window locations. Here are plants for warm rooms, cool rooms, rooms with plenty of space. I have included plants commonly sold by florists and rarer plants that are bound to be a challenge. These are mainly "greenhouse" plants, but with a little extra attention I have been able to get them to bloom in the house; and very likely you can, too. There have been countless other plants that did not adapt to my conditions; these have not been included. But it is quite possible that they might bloom beautifully for you; my failures could be your successes.

Doubtless I have omitted some of your favorites, a matter of space rather than dislike. In any case, I have presented a selection of plants to bring color to your home throughout the year. I hope these flowering house plants will bring you as much pleasure as they have brought me.

JACK KRAMER

Chicago, Illinois

Contents

ix

APPENDIX

BIBLIOGRAPHY

INDEX

Illustrations

Part I *A Year of Flowering House Plants*

1

MEDINILLA MAGNIFICA (above)
NEOMARICA GRACILIS (below)

1

January

JANUARY is gray and snowy in the Midwest, and color at the window does much to lighten spirits and bring cheer to the house. A flowering plant on the dining table or in the living room is a happy sight; and although some plants are dormant now, others are in full bloom.

FOR WARM ROOMS (68°-78° F.)

Anthurium Scherzerianum, the Flamingo Plant, has a showy, lacquered, coral-red spathe that looks artificial, perhaps because it lasts for five months. Coming from jungles in Central and South America, Anthuriums need high humidity and warmth. Pot them in an osmunda fiber–sphagnum mixture and water heavily—every day in summer, somewhat less often the rest of the year.

Asparagus Sprengeri, Asparagus-Fern or Needle Asparagus, occupies the west corner of my plant room; it is graceful and airy, with great weeping-willow branches of ferny emerald-green. It blooms sporadically throughout the year: tiny, fragrant, blush-white flowers are followed by pink berries on a cascading scape. Water it liberally, then allow it to dry out before wetting again. Occasionally I snip branches to arrange with cut flowers; they make lovely backgrounds. Don't overlook this plant—it's a dandy—but start with a big specimen if you want bloom, for small ones rarely flower. It is decorative and grows under almost any light conditions.

Begonia 'Bow-Arriola' is a rhizomatous miniature, really a "mighty mite," with star-shaped leaves of satiny green with purple markings. Flowers are pink and pretty, and the plant needs little space at the window. Pot in a shallow container and grow it on the dry side. Winter sunlight is essential for bloom.

Billbergia nutans, Queen's Tears, is the Bromeliad of the month, and a better house plant is hard to find. Fast growing, floriferous, and with one of the most brilliant color combinations in the floral world—green, pink, and blue—this plant is easily seen across a room. Unlike most members of the Pineapple family, *B. nutans* has green grasslike leaves without prominent spines. Grow it in a terrestrial mix (Chapter 13) with sand added, and let the roots fill the pot. Moisture all year, bright light, and good humidity pay off with a colorful display. This Bromeliad can be grown in pots outdoors in areas where temperatures stay above 50° F. at night.

Jacobinia Ghiesbreghtiana, King's Crowns, is an evergreen with terminal clusters of vivid orange-crimson flowers. With one raceme opening after another, a plant blooms for about six weeks. Jacobinias wilt without daily watering in hot weather, so drench the soil throughout the summer. Other species in the family that make good house plants are *J. carnea*, with pink flowers appearing in late spring, and *J. suberecta*, with orange blooms in July. Sunshine is essential for all of them.

Manettia bicolor, the Candy-Corn Plant, blooms its head off in the house. And what a delightful small plant it is, with red-and-yellow flowers that look like the Halloween confection. This charming climber likes full light rather than direct sun, and grows exuberantly in an airy place. It blooms best when slightly pot-bound and requires plenty of water. An easy, cheerful plant. Don't miss this one.

For Cool Rooms (52°-68° F.)

Neomarica gracilis, the Apostle Plant, is graceful, fragrant, and dependable; its long, tapered foliage and white, brown, and blue flowers make it look very like an Iris. After blooms fade, new plants form in the sheath. Although flowers last but a few days, each fan produces three or four. Grow plants in small pots of sandy soil and give them plenty of light and moisture. Other excellent species are *N. Northiana*, with white flowers, and the blue *N. caerulea*. It wouldn't be winter to me without an Apostle plant at the window.

Odontoglossum grande, the popular Tiger Orchid, is sure to bloom in your home with sunlight, good humidity, and a long rest (about a month) without water, before and after flowering. The inflorescence is 5 inches across, vivid yellow and brown, and lasts three weeks. This medium-sized grower bears flowers year after year for me. To encourage budding, set it outdoors through September and into October as long as night temperatures remain in the high forties. You might also like the much smaller *O. pulchellum*, with white flowers and Lily-of-the-Valley fragrance. Plant either one in slotted clay pots with fir bark (Chapter 13).

2

MANETTIA BICOLOR

Oxalis is a workhorse of the indoor garden, and many varieties bloom lavishly with little care. I grow them indiscriminately and have eight pots, continually adding more. This month, *O. hirta* is bright with deep rose-red flowers, the centers stained yellow. Pot up the tubers, three to a 5-inch pot, in early fall and water sparingly until growth starts. Then increase moisture. After a plant blooms, let it rest without water in a cool place. There are a number of kinds of Oxalis suitable for the sunny indoor garden. Many, like *O. melanosticta*, are dormant in spring and summer but bear yellow flowers in fall. Then there are the yellow *O. Ortgiesii*, *O. cernua* and the pink *O. rosea*, all beautiful.

Zygocactus truncatus (*Schlumbergera*) is the Crab, or Christmas Cactus, and most of the plants we get are hybrids. In my house, this cactus is glorious in a 10-inch pot with hundreds of pendent crimson flowers. I dry it out somewhat for four weeks in September or October to encourage holiday blooming, and through autumn give it direct sun and high humidity. 'Gertrude Beahm' is a red hybrid, and there are lavender varieties, too. All make splendid house plants. A specimen Christmas Cactus in bloom is a veritable fountain of color.

FOR BASKET AND BRACKET

Chlorophytum elatum, the Spider Plant, thrives in a 10-inch pot set into a 6-foot iron stand in the northwest corner of my living room. A hanging plant, this bears small lily-like flowers on runners that are sometimes 3 to 4 feet long; the runner tips produce plantlets. Roots soon fill a pot, so supply a large container at the start; in a few months you will have a lovely display. I call it the "friendship plant" because so many people request cuttings; these root readily in water. The Spider Plant grows under almost any light conditions and can be neglected for days because its roots have water-storage vessels.

Rhipsalis burchelli is an unusual Cactus with green pencil-like "leaves" and rose-colored flowers followed by bright berries. Excellent for a basket, this is easy to grow, and even small plants bear flowers. My large plant is effective in a bracket between windows. Coming from jungles, this Cactus requires heat and humidity. Also worth space indoors are *R. capilliformis* and *R. paradoxa*, both with white flowers.

FOR A CHALLENGE

Allium neapolitanum, the Flowering Onion, bears starry white flowers in 3-inch umbels and has slender leaves. Often grown in gardens, it also blooms well in the house when given sun and heavy watering. Plant bulbs in October, one to a 6-inch pot, and grow cold, with scanty moisture, for about two months. Then increase moisture and set plants in a warm window.

IF YOU HAVE ROOM

Medinilla magnifica is a big, handsome shrub with thick, leathery leaves having white midribs. The panicle of red flowers with purple anthers and pink bracts is indeed showy. Grow this plant in west light with good moisture and warmth, and wash the foliage frequently in the sink. It takes a mature specimen to bloom, so this plant is for those with perseverance.

FROM THE FLORIST

Azalea from the genus Rhodendron is a stunning plant. In many different colors, Azaleas are always welcome guests. The trick is to make them permanent residents, and this really isn't too difficult. Color lasts from January until March; oc-

casional misting of leaves, a cool place (below 65° F.), and
moist soil are needed. After flowers fade, dry out the plants
somewhat until warm weather. In May, put them outside on
a porch or sink them into a garden bed. Resume regular watering and spray foliage daily. With this treatment, I have
carried over three pots of Azaleas from year to year. For me,
these fine flowering plants are the indoor roses of the garden
world and I wouldn't be without them. Many forms available, all good.

Begonia X cheimantha is one of the Christmas Begonias.
If you received it last year as a gift, it should be bright now
with nodding pink flowers. To carry plants over, grow them
rather cool at night (under 65° F.) and somewhat moist all
year. After they bloom, cut tops back severely and set plants
in a warm place, say about 72° F. at night. When new shoots
appear at the base of a plant, you can cut them off and root
them in a propagating case—an inexpensive way to have
Christmas Begonias next year.

STILL COLORFUL

Aechmea racinae	(December—February)
Calanthe vestita hybrids	(November—February)
Camellia varieties	(November—March)
Eranthemum nervosum	(November—March)
Euphorbia pulcherrima	(December—January)

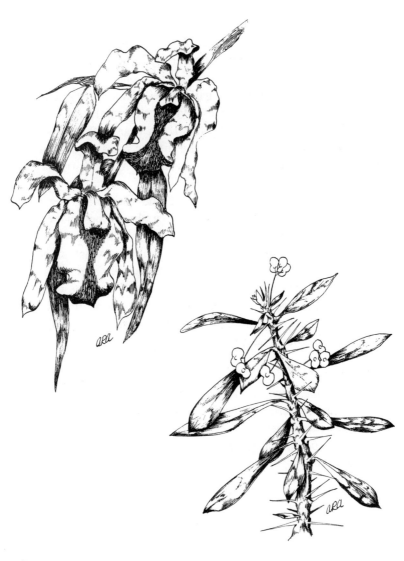

3

COELOGYNE CRISTATA (above)
EUPHORBIA SPLENDENS (below)

2

February

FEBRUARY is usually very cold and cloudy. Outside, nature seems at a standstill, but indoors many house plants are starting into growth—a new shoot here, a green leaf there. Some of my favorites are put under fluorescent light now for necessary "sunshine." Others are moved away from frigid windows, and there is a small electric heater in the corner of the plant room for emergency use. It is wise now to watch the watering schedule; too many cloudy days with too much water will kill plants.

FOR WARM ROOMS (68°-78° F.)

Aechmea angustifolia, a Bromeliad, bears a tall pendent scape of flowers of an unusual, hard-to-find shade of blue, followed by small blue berries. The display lasts until April. Like most Aechmeas, this is undemanding. Moderate watering, some sun, and an occasional misting of the leaves spell success. Pot in a 3- or 4-inch container in osmunda fiber, and you can sit back and enjoy this obliging plant.

Echeveria Derenbergii is a small plant often sold as a Cactus; actually, it is a Crassula, and an excellent flowering one. The inflorescence is orange-red on short spikes, several to a plant. It grows readily with little care, but be sure to reduce watering in winter. Many varieties available.

Euphorbia splendens, Crown-of-Thorns, has traveled with me from one apartment to another for twelve years. It is now old and big, but I can't part with it even though I hardly have room for it. However, most Euphorbias are of medium size; and these are dependable plants. The red bracts surround tiny, cheery yellow flowers that appear more or less freely, depending on sunlight. Provide small pots of light, rich, porous soil and grow rather dry all year, for these are desert plants. Severe changes of temperature or drafts are harmful. Easily trained to a pot trellis and effective grown this way.

Oncidium ampliatum is usually the first Orchid of the year to bloom on the sun porch; the small yellow flowers on a pendent scape look brighter still against a gray sky. This is a reliable plant and gives much pleasure for little care; it seems just too tough to kill. After it blooms, I carry it dry until late April; new growth starts then and I increase watering as leaves expand. In hot weather, I water it heavily and place it at a south window. The handsome floral sprays are also effective when cut and put in a vase of water; they last about a month.

For Cool Rooms (52°-68° F.)

Coelogyne cristata, an Orchid from the Himalayas, is now a cascade of snow-white flowers with yellow throats. Neglect this plant to get bloom; over-watering kills it. It needs sun and good humidity. To be sure of flowers, put it outside in August. Leave it there through cool (but frost-free) nights. Take it in in late October (unless frost comes sooner) and dry it out somewhat before starting regular watering again. Pot in fir bark (Chapter 13).

Daphne odora, 'Fragrant Daphne', is sweetly scented; it is a lovely plant with glossy, dark-green leaves and clusters of star-shaped, white-to-purple flowers. It needs to be grown cool until mid-December. I have my plant at a south window in an unheated pantry at about 48° F. at night. After mid-December I move it to the cool end of my plant room in bright light. Because its roots do not tolerate soggy conditions, pot Daphne in a sandy soil and make sure of drainage. The variegated form, *D. odora marginata*, has white-edged leaves.

Pelargonium 'Alphonse Ricard' is but one of a number of wonderful Geraniums to brighten a house in winter. This is a large grower with magnificent red flowers. It requires cool nights, 48° to 55° F. Soak soil well, then allow it to dry out somewhat between waterings. Although not reputed to be easy, this geranium has grown beautifully for me.

Reinwardtia indica, Yellow Flax, is a medium-sized plant with dark-green leaves and large yellow flowers that look like petunias. Blooms appear at the tips of shoots on and off from November until Easter, but most abundantly this month. In time plants become straggly, so pinch off shoots occasionally to induce nice shapely growth. My plant is in an 8-inch pot in a cool, airy place at a south window. This is a beautiful plant you are sure to enjoy.

For Basket and Bracket

Begonia 'Limminghei' is pendent flowering, with pointed shiny green leaves and clusters of coral-red flowers. The plant

4

ECHEVERIA

needs warmth (72° F.), bright light, and good moisture all year. It soon fills a basket and offers a brilliant display at eye level. Grow this popular Begonia; it gives complete satisfaction.

Lantana montevidensis in a wire basket occupies the southwest corner of my plant room. This lavender-flowered species grows and blooms freely when given frequent watering plus sun and warmth. It makes a colorful decoration for little effort.

For a Challenge

Sparmannia africana, sometimes called Indoor Linden, is worth the small extra effort it requires. Flowers are white with yellow stamens and are very attractive and long lasting. Pot in average soil and pinch out young shoots a few times while the plant is growing. In winter, give full sun; water heavily all year except for a few weeks right after flowering, when a rest period is needed.

If You Have Room

Arthropodium cirrhatum, with tall spikes of white flowers and attractive foliage, is a New Zealand member of the Lily family that requires considerable moisture while it is growing. After plants bloom, keep soil somewhat dry. A cool west window, high humidity, and a 50° F. temperature make this an easy-to-grow plant.

From the Florist

Cyclamen, with large nodding flowers in white, pink, or red, is almost irresistible at this season. Cyclamens are glamorous but difficult for me to keep for more than a month. Select plants with many buds rather than open flowers and put in a cool place. (In the greenhouse, they were grown at

50° F.) Drench daily; these are really thirsty plants. After flowering, if you want to try and hold them over, reduce watering; then, in spring, plunge them in a shady part of the garden. Water well through the summer and repot in August. Then place at a sunny window and hope for the best.

STILL COLORFUL

Anthurium Scherzerianum	(January—April)
Manettia bicolor	(January—March)
Oxalis cernua	(February—May)
Zygocactus truncatus varieties	(January—February)

3

March

Rᴀɪɴ, wind, and gray skies are the insignia of March, and the spring awakening we hardly notice outdoors is evident in our indoor plants. Small green shoots appear and the growing area seems more alive. This is a busy month for indoor gardeners. Pot bulbs for future flowering, make cuttings of your prize plants for gifts, repot husky growers, and spray with an insecticide to ward off pests that may appear now. Open the windows a little, as weather permits, to let in fresh air.

Fᴏʀ Wᴀʀᴍ Rᴏᴏᴍs (68°-78° F.)

Aechmea chantinii, queen of Bromeliads, welcomes spring with a branched spike of fiery-red bracts crowned in yellow —a stunning inflorescence. The olive-green leaves that form

17

5

ABUTILON (above)
HELICONIA PSITTACORUM (below)

the vase are banded in gray. Humidity, moderate watering, and some sunshine are required. Pot Aechmeas in small containers of osmunda fiber. A superlative house plant, with or without bloom.

Begonia coccinea is everblooming, but it is at its best now with clusters of red flowers cascading over silver-spotted green leaves. Grow it on the dry side throughout the year, and be sure it has winter sun—it will not bloom without it. At this time, move it from a south to a west exposure. This plant offers a really lusty show of color.

Epidendrum stamfordianum is a spray Orchid that needs little care to produce dainty yellow-and-red flowers, hundreds to a bunch, with three or four tiny bouquets on each plant. Quite a show. This graceful epiphyte must have a complete rest after flowering, four to six weeks at least. Water it as growth starts and increase moisture through the summer. Pot in fir bark (Chapter 13) and grow in the sun. This is but one of many Epidendrums available; most of them are good house plants.

Musa velutina, a dwarf Banana, is well suited to home culture. From 36 to 44 inches tall, it makes a great vertical accent for the corner of a room. The large spoon-shaped leaves and the erect red bracts with yellow flowers are indeed handsome. Winter sun and summer shade are necessary, as is liberal moisture through the year. Banana trees do not drop leaves and pruning is unnecessary, but don't expect fruit. Also available is the slightly smaller *M. nana*.

Strobilanthes isophyllus, from India, has dark, evergreen leaves with clusters of pretty lavender flowers. It starts to bloom when quite young and needs warmth, humidity, and sun. It reminds me of an upright willow tree, and I find it a good grower for my plant room. For best results, cut it back severely in December.

For Cool Rooms (52°-68° F.)

Abutilon, the Flowering-Maple, is becoming increasingly popular, and it is indeed a pretty house plant. Related to the Hollyhock, Abutilons have maple-like leaves and paper-thin bell flowers. There are many hybrids, with flowers in delicate shades of yellow, orange, red—all hard to resist. Grow these at a south or west exposure and water heavily in warm weather; they will not tolerate dryness at any time. I usually make fresh cuttings every year because old plants tend to get straggly. Sun is essential, and a rich soil is fine for potting. To insure bloom, keep plants pot-bound.

Acacia armata, the Kangaroo-Thorn from Australia, has dark-green leaves and pretty yellow flowers. My plant, with three arching branches, makes a handsome table decoration. Acacias need plenty of sun and water and a cold place; 45° F. is fine. *A. Baileyana*, somewhat larger, has silvery, fernlike foliage and yellow flowers.

Citrus taitensis, the popular dwarf Otaheite Orange, as well as other citrus plants, now appears in supermarkets and florists' shops. The shiny green bushes are easy to grow, and the delicate white flowers are heavily scented. If you hand-pollinate the blossoms you might get a few fruits. Otherwise, be content with the plant; it is handsome and decorative. Provide a rich soil and water heavily, except in winter. Bright light keeps Citrus plants a healthy green. To discourage attacks of red spider, spray foliage occasionally with an all-purpose insecticide.

For Basket and Bracket

Chorizema cordatum prefers to climb rather than trail. Either way, it is a show-off, with holly-like leaves and red flowers that look like Sweet Peas. Bright sun, a poor soil, and coolness encourage a lovely, colorful display. Pinch back young plants to promote sturdy growth.

Mahernia verticillata, Honey Bells, with brilliant sweet-scented golden flowers, is always welcome on the unheated, but not freezing, sun porch. A well-grown specimen produces a cascade of color. Full sun, high humidity, and constant moisture bring it into bloom this month. You can make new plants from spring-rooted cuttings.

For a Challenge

Cytisus canariensis brings bright yellow to the window garden with a wealth of pea-shaped blossoms. Prune plants occasionally to make them shapely. High humidity and full sun are needed for flowering. Pot in sandy soil and grow cool; my plant thrives in an unheated pantry (45° to 50° F. at night). Not easy, but a delight in bloom this dark month.

If You Have Room

Heliconia, with leaves like the Banana, has been an ideal house plant for me without special attention, and I would not be without it. I admire the large decorative leaves and unusual flowers, which always attract my visitors. My rules for success are quantities of water and plenty of heat and humidity except in winter, when plants rest somewhat. *H. psittacorum* blooms for me this month; its orange-and-blue flowers suggest the Bird-of-Paradise plant. I also like *H. aurantiaca,* with orange-and-green bracts and red flowers, and *H. angustifolia,* with red bracts and white flowers, which blooms in October. Don't be afraid to try these if you have enough space. They do beautifully in a sunny window.

From the Florist

Calceolaria, the Pouch Flower, with its gay array of colors, is seen in most flower shops this month. Plants have thin green

6

EUCHARIS GRANDIFLORA

leaves and clusters of showy flowers with an inflated lower lip in shades of yellow or orange with red or maroon spots. This annual will be with you for only a few weeks after bloom starts, so culture is simple: moderate warmth and good moisture. Calceolarias cannot be carried over from year to year, but you can start new plants from seed.

STILL COLORFUL

Aechmea angustifolia	(February—May)
Begonia 'Limminghei'	(January—May)
Euphorbia splendens	(February—April)
Oncidium ampliatum	(February—March)
Lantana montevidensis	(February—April)

4

April

April is rain and sun and a springtime feeling. In the indoor garden, we sense the awakening of the outside world in our flowering plants. Many are in bloom and others are budding with the color that is to come. This is a good time to move the sun-lovers to west and east windows and to groom plants for the summer ahead. There are even a few cold-tolerant Bromeliads and Orchids that can be put outdoors at the end of the month if you need the indoor space.

For Warm Rooms (68°-78° F.)

Crossandra infundibuliformis is a long name for a delightful small plant, an evergreen from India, with masses of bright orange flowers in overlapping clusters. Although it blooms into summer, Crossandra is at its best now. The shiny green leaves are attractive and, although the plants are often con-

7

SPREKELIA FORMOSISSIMA (above)
IXORA (below)

sidered difficult, I have found them easy. My plant is on a kitchen window sill where there is good air circulation. A thirsty plant, it needs water every day all year. A few hours of sunshine are fine, and an occasional spraying of the foliage is beneficial.

Eucharis grandiflora, the Amazon-Lily to me is a riddle plant. I'm never sure when it is going to bloom, but from my experience, April is the most likely time to expect flowers. The broad, shiny leaves appear lacquered and the white inflorescence glows like snowflakes. The fragrance is sweet and pleasing. Blooms come after a few months of rapid growth with liberal watering. After it flowers, water sparingly for about a month, then resume a regular schedule. Sunlight, high humidity, and a rich soil are required for bloom. This is popular for arrangements.

Dendrobium Pierardii is an Orchid that is fast becoming a popular house plant. This dependable species welcomes April with blush-pink flowers, two or three to a node on a pendent scape. A good basket plant, it can also be trained to grow vertically by staking. Water it heavily from April through September, when it is in growth. Then dry it out in a cooler place (about 55° F.) until February, when buds appear. Resume watering then and find a sunny window for this epiphyte. *D. Chrysotoxom* also handsome, handle same way.

Ixora is a pleasant surprise in the indoor garden. The first small plants I bought years ago, with a few flowers apiece, were hardly an indication of the magnificent hybrids to come. My Ixoras bloom twice, once this month and then again in June, with heavy crowns of red, orange, or yellow flowers. These sturdy house plants need only bright light and water, and even one plant dresses up a room. *I. coccinea, I. chinensis,* and *I. javanica* produce red flowers. For heavy bloom and radiant color try the hybrids, especially 'Gillette's Yellow,' a real winner.

Passiflora alato-caerulea, the popular Passion Flower, is not easy to grow in the home; but if you can coax it to produce only one flower, it is worth the effort. Blooms measure over 5 inches across and are a startling blue. This is the cultural program I have followed: I transferred the original plant to a 6-inch pot and then, about a month later, I provided a 10-inch pot of greenhouse soil with a liberal amount of shards for drainage. I cut back young shoots frequently to promote strong growth and once a week apply a liquid fertilizer. I water heavily from early March on, and the plant grows rapidly at a south window, first flowers appearing this month. For best results, keep a Passiflora in the same pot after the 10-inch size is reached and top-dress the soil about once a year. Also interesting is *P. coccinea*, a fiery red.

For Cool Rooms (52°-68° F.)

Dietes, a member of the Iris family, is often sold as *Moraea*. The latter, however, grows from a corm, while Dietes grows from a rhizome and retains its leaves. Although flowers last only a day or so, they are produced continually for a week or more. Keep the plant at a sunny window and, when it is actively growing, water heavily. *D. bicolor* has yellow flowers, *D. catenulata*, white.

Sprekelia formosissima, the Aztec-Lily, grows from a bulb. Pot it in winter or early spring; do not divide it thereafter, but allow the pot to become crowded. The solitary crimson flower appears before leaf growth. A sunny window is needed for success. Let the soil dry out between waterings.

Streptocarpus Rexii, the Cape-Primrose, has lovely blue flowers. This Gesneriad needs good drainage and plenty of winter sun. The inflorescence is much like that of the Gloxinia; the foliage is coarse and green. The hybrids are excellent, with blue, pink, white, or purple flowers. They bloom over a long period in spring and summer.

For Basket and Bracket

Aristolochia elegans, the Calico Flower, is a curiosity with odd-shaped, floppy, pouchlike flowers of green, spotted brown. This strange plant grows rapidly in warm weather, but it can be kept to reasonable size by cutting back. It needs full sun, high humidity, and copious watering except in winter. Although not very pretty, it is worth growing and children love it. Other species are better suited to the greenhouse than the window sill.

Columnea hirta, another Gesneriad, dazzles the eye with a fountain of brilliant orange flowers. Such epiphytes from the jungles are very floriferous and grow well in the warmth and humidity I provide for my Orchids. For striking color you might also grow *C. arguta*, with red flowers; *C. microphylla*, red and yellow; and *C. tulae* 'Flava,' yellow.

For a Challenge

Gazania rigens accents a window with black-eyed orange daisies. It is a vigorous plant for a cool, sunny location. Keep the soil on the dry side and summer the plants in the garden if you can. In August, take cuttings for new plants. There are many splendid hybrids in bright red and orange.

Stephanotis floribunda, Madagascar-Jasmine, glistens with waxy white, sweet-scented flowers from April to August. Foliage is glossy green and attractive. Provide a warm place at a west window; syringe foliage daily in hot weather. Cut back after flowering and rest the plant for about a month around October or November. Keep in the same pot for several years and topdress the soil annually.

If You Have Room

Aechmea fulgens var. *discolor*, a Bromeliad with a rosette of green leaves, is purple beneath and covered with gray

8

STEPHANOTIS FLORIBUNDA

crossbands above. Tiny violet flowers are followed by red berries that last through summer. Pot in a 6-inch container with osmunda fiber and give warmth, humidity, and good moisture. Be sure to keep the "cup" filled with water, and spray the foliage occasionally. Sunshine turns leaves a brilliant purple, a striking color with the red fruit. A handsome plant for indoors or the patio.

Clivia miniata, the Kafir-Lily, was one of my first tropicals. In bloom this commands attention with its clusters of orange flowers cupped in dark-green, straplike leaves. Grown from a bulb, Clivia is an excellent house plant for any large window. For bloom, keep pot-bound and topdress soil yearly. Do not pamper by overwatering; neglect brings the flowers. Although you can start bulbs yourself, it is better to buy a mature plant. These aristocrats of the Amaryllis family are highly recommended for indoors. The newer Belgian and English hybrids are robust growers.

FROM THE FLORIST

Cineraria (*Senecio cruentus*), with daisy-like flowers in shades of blue, is hard to resist. I always buy a pot, knowing too well the flowers will last only a few weeks in the house. Still, the dramatic color seems worth the expenditure. To keep plants as long as possible, grow cool (about 55° F.) and water heavily.

STILL COLORFUL

Begonia coccinea	(March—June)
Heliconia species	(March—July)
Strobilanthes isophyllus	(March—June)
Abutilon hybrids	(March—June)
Aechmea chantinii	(March—June)

5

May

THIS month the indoor garden glows; many plants are in bloom and others are actively growing. Cut back the tropicals to strengthen them, and topdress any tub specimens. Mist the air several times a day to increase humidity, and arrange pots at the windows to allow for summer light; the sun is high now and at a different angle from in winter. Some species can go outside at this time or be sunk in pots in the garden. In the Midwest, growth is just starting outdoors but the indoor garden is already full of life.

FOR WARM ROOM (68°-78° F.)

Acalypha hispida, the Chenille Plant, decorative and unusual, starts the month. The bright pink flowers grow like

31

9

ACALYPHA HISPIDA (above)
TIBOUCHINA SEMIDECANDRA (below)

strings and are 4 to 6 inches long. Shade from hot sun in summer; but the rest of the year grow it in bright light with high humidity. It requires moderate watering throughout the year.

Begonia 'Ricinifolia,' with rhizomatous roots, has foliage that suggests the Castor-Bean plant. When only a year old it produces lovely pink flowers, and the large star-shaped leaves are lavish and attractive. Grow it on the dry side all year, with winter sun and summer shading. In late fall my plant drops leaves but recovers in a few months. This Begonia responds well to artificial light.

Crassula triebnerii is a small, beautiful plant with pale-green leaves, toothed and dotted. White flowers crown a tall stalk to brighten a room. These plants will stand neglect and still survive, but for flowers, provide a sandy soil and moderate watering. There are more than twenty Crassulas available; all make good house plants.

Guzmania monostachia is graceful, attractive, and dependable for bloom. This Bromeliad is a fountain of lush green leaves topped with a thrusting flower head of brilliant red, white, and deep green—an arresting color combination. It needs little attention other than moderate watering. Pot in a 4-inch container of osmunda fiber (Chapter 13) and give some sun.

Tibouchina semidecandra, the Glory Bush, lights a window with purple flowers that last only a day but are quickly replaced by others. The pale-green, hairy leaves turn red as they mature. Although this is actually a shrub, it thrives in a 6-inch pot at a west window. Occasionally I pinch off branches to keep my plant shapely. A healthy specimen blooms from May to September.

For Cool Rooms (52°-68° F.)

Haemanthus Katharinae, the Blood-Lily, deserves space in

every large collection. The inflorescence is spectacular—a sphere of red flowers on an erect stalk. Grown from a bulb, the plant blooms after the leaves mature. Pot one bulb to a 6- or 8-inch container, with the top of the bulb slightly above the soil line. Give little water at the start but more as growth develops. Syringe foliage frequently, and grow the plant in full sun. *H. coccineus* is also attractive, with large drooping leaves and red flowers in autumn. It is said the blooms are followed by blue berries, but I have yet to see these on my plants.

Rosa chinensis var. *minima*, a miniature Rose, offers tiny duplicates of the hybrid teas, and is a delight to grow at home. Plants take up little room and in full sun bloom freely through the fall. Water moderately and feed every other week. After blooming cut plants back to 4 inches and store cool, about 45° F. In late January return plants to a sunny window. There are many varieties, with flowers of white, yellow, pink, rose, red, lavender, and various shades in between.

Vallota speciosa, the Scarborough-Lily, is an Amaryllis with 2-inch scarlet flowers. It grows and blooms with little attention and the handsome plant is attractive all year. Perfect drainage is essential, stagnant water not being tolerated, although ample moisture is required. Even when plants are resting in winter, the soil should be almost wet. My plant bears flowers with only morning sun. Grow Vallotas in the same pot for several years.

For Basket and Bracket

Bougainvillea, a woody vine with bracts of vivid color, brightens the indoor garden now if there is plenty of sun. Plants can crowd you out of space because they are robust growers. Feed and water liberally until October, then reduce

1-FUCHSIA, STELLAR BASKET PLANT *(above)*
2-THE AUTHOR'S PLANT ROOM *(below)*

3-AN IDEAL DWARF POT PLANT, AGAPANTHUS 'PETER PAN'   *(above)*
4-THE POPULAR CHRISTMAS CACTUS, ZYGOCACTUS HYBRID   *(below)*

10

VALLOTA SPECIOSA

moisture; after flowering, cut Bougainvilleas back and grow them warm. Don't make the mistake (as I once did) of summering this vine outdoors where it can entwine itself around a post; by fall I couldn't get it back into the house. When watering, soak plants well and then allow them to dry out before watering again. There are varieties with blooms of white, purple, red, salmon, and yellow.

Cyanotis somaliensis, Pussy Ears, from tropical Africa, takes little space and is attractive, with purple flowers and white-haired leaves. Grow plants warm with high humidity and good moisture all year. For a nice showing, group several plants in one container. Although not outstanding, these are pleasant fill-ins for the growing area.

FOR A CHALLENGE

Petrea volubilis, Queen's Wreath, is worth a try; it takes patience to bring this beauty into bloom. Here is how I did it: I shifted the original small plant to a 6-inch pot and, after a month, to an 8-inch tub of rich soil with some bone meal. I placed it on the floor at a southeast exposure and watered it heavily through the summer, giving a liquid feeding every second week. It was three years before the stunning clouds of blue flowers appeared, but they were worth waiting for. They hang from the tips of the branches against long, elliptical wavy leaves. This plant is big but glorious in bloom and deserves its pretty common name of Queen's Wreath.

IF YOU HAVE ROOM

Dendrobium densiflorum, an Orchid with cane growth and handsome leathery foliage, has an inflorescence which in bud looks like a cluster of grapes. Within two weeks the buds open into a dazzling display of yellow flowers, a truly stunning sight. Plants need warmth when growing but coolness

11

PETREA VOLUBILIS

from November until January to encourage budding. At night a 15° drop from day temperature is good. Give a complete rest, without any water, during the winter. Start to water again in January and return the plant to its former sunny window. This Orchid requires full sun all year and good air circulation. Although more difficult to grow at home than most Dendrobiums, a plant in flower is a real reward. Buy a large specimen, one with 3- to 4-foot canes.

FROM THE FLORIST

Hydrangea appears now, with pink or blue flowers, and I am told that it can be carried over. However, I have never tried to do this. This plant needs water twice a day in summer. If you want to try to keep it after flowering, cut it back severely and repot. Then plunge the pot in the garden and feed when growth starts. After frost, bring plants to a cool place and keep roots somewhat dry. Through February, grow at 50° F. Then move to a warm, sunny window. Water and hope for flowers.

STILL COLORFUL

Columnea hybrids	(April—July)
Crossandra infundibuliformis	(April—August)
Dendrobium Pierardii	(April—May)
Ixora hybrids	(March—July)
Passiflora alato-caerulea	(April—June)
Streptocarpus Rexii	(April—July)

6

June

JUNE is the time to put in window screens for shading and to set more plants outdoors for refreshing rains. Tropicals like Heliconias and Gingers can be put on the porch for a summer sojourn. This is a good month to determine which plants are thriving and to discard those that are merely getting along. Every year, because of limitations of space I am forced either to throw away unresponsive specimens or to make a last attempt to stimulate them with some time outdoors. Color is rampant at the windows now and the repotting and pruning and care given the plants through the winter bring dividends in a rich harvest of flowers.

FOR WARM ROOMS (52°-68° F.)

Aphelandra aurantiaca Roezlii is the showiest member of

39

APHELANDRA AURANTIACA ROEZLII
(above)
KAEMPFERIA ROSCOEANA (below)

the genus. With gray-green leaves, it produces an arresting triangular orange crown of flowers that lasts a month. Heavy watering and high humidity with sunlight make this plant a lovely showpiece. *A. chamissoniana*, from the florist, is attractive, too, with bright yellow flowers and leaves with ivory midrib and veins. Another excellent species is *A. squarrosa Louisae*, with bright-green foliage and yellow flowers.

Kaempferia roscoeana, the Resurrection-Lily, is a gem. I cannot think of a better flowering plant than this Ginger. The attractive spoon-shaped leaves are embroidered in green and purple, a perfect background for the lavender flower that appears daily. Although lasting only twenty-four hours, it is quickly replaced by another flower next morning. My plant had about sixty flowers in six weeks, and I hardly knew where they came from. They seemed to sprout overnight from the leaf axils. Water heavily until blossoming stops; then store the plant at 60° F. and repot next March. A west window is ideal, or put this plant on the kitchen window sill where it can be fully appreciated.

Kohleria, like the African-Violet, has velvety leaves. Even when young this excellent Gesneriad produces highly colored tubular flowers, cheerful and bright. Ample sun in fall and winter helps to create a colorful display. Good moisture is needed all year, but keep water off the leaves. Grow Kohlerias into large specimen plants; they are effective this way. *K. amabilis* has pink flowers; *K. bogotensis*, red and yellow; and *K. eriantha*, a larger type, red.

Lockhartia Oerstedii is the strange Braided Orchid that always interests the visitors to my plant room. It is not so dramatic as many orchids, but it has a quiet charm and grows with little attention. The green, overlapping foliage accounts for the common name, and the tiny yellow-and-red flowers are quite pleasing. Grow it in fir bark (Chapter 13) and water only twice a week; a west location is ideal.

13

KOHLERIA

Vriesea splendens, a popular Bromeliad called Flaming Sword, is an excellent plant although it is not so spectacular as some other Bromeliads. It has green leaves striped mahogany, and bears a tall, flat, bright-orange flower head—hence the common name. The inflorescence lasts for months and the plant requires little care. It blooms readily at a north window.

FOR COOL ROOMS (52°-68° F.)

Alstroemeria pulchella, the Brazilian-Lily, always surprises me. I never expect the weedy, unattractive specimen I buy to bloom, but it always does. It has lovely red-and-green flowers on a tall stem, really quite pretty. Water plants sparingly and bring them into growth slowly, shading them from summer sun. My plant is in a 10-inch pot and is summered in the garden. After foliage fades, keep soil somewhat dry until April.

Russelia equisetiformis, the Coral Plant, is adorned with clusters of red flowers. It grows to about 4 feet, with light-green foliage. Give this shrub some sun, and water sparingly all year. Prune in early spring.

Tulbaghia fragrans offers a great spray of fragrant pink flowers and blooms readily in sun. Related to Agapanthus, this plant has evergreen leaves, and it is easy to grow. Pot three or four corms half an inch deep and an inch apart in sandy soil in a 6-inch container. Give plenty of water and feeding.

FOR BASKET AND BRACKET

Aeschynanthus speciosus (*Trichosporum*), is a dazzling trailing epiphyte from the Asian tropics. Decorative and vivid, its flowers are usually orange-red. Rich soil, perfect drainage, and high humidity keep it healthy; I grow my plant

with the Orchids. Warmth—never less than 62° F. at night—
and sun are essential for bloom.

Schizocentron elegans, the Spanish-Shawl Plant, is small and
attractive, with a mass of red flowers and green leaves on red
stems. It thrives in a cool, sunny window with constant
moisture and high humidity.

For a Challenge

Dipladenia amoena should decorate every plant room. This
lovely tropical vine with pink funnel-shaped flowers is sweetly
scented and has handsome foliage, crinkly and dark green.
Unfortunately, it takes patience to coax plants to bloom;
mainly, they need full sun and high humidity. This did the
trick for me.

If You Have Room

Clerodendrum Thompsoniae earns the name Glory Bower,
for it is a stunning plant covered with white bracts and red
flowers. A robust grower, it drops leaves in winter when resting. Reduce water at this time and, if possible, move to a
cool place (58° F. at night). When it is growing provide full
sun, liberal water, and high humidity. My plant bloomed a
second time two months after the first flowering. Although it
is a shrub that can grow to 10 feet, even an 18-inch plant will
bloom. *C. fragrans* is bushy, with white flowers; *C. Bungei*
has rose-red blooms.

Nerium Oleander, the familiar Oleander, puts on a grand
show from now until fall. There are many varieties with
either single or double flowers in shades of yellow, pink, red,
and white. The willowy stems with pointed green leaves are
a perfect foil for the showy racemes. I have grown many
Oleanders under various conditions. For success I suggest
coolness (about 52° F. at night), copious watering, and a

14

DIPLADENIA AMOENA

15

CLERODENDRUM THOMPSONIAE

summer outside. Although mine are tub specimens, even small plants bloom.

FROM THE FLORIST

Gloxinia (*Sinningia*) is an exquisite flowering plant and hard to resist. Unlike many gift plants, Gloxinias can be kept colorful for weeks with just a little care. Keep them cool and well watered in a shaded window. The bell-shaped blooms are rich blue, purple, violet, rose, red, or white. Some are spotted. After flowers fade, store the tubers in the pots at 60° F.; water only occasionally. When new growth starts, repot in fresh soil and bring back to the window.

STILL COLORFUL

Begonia 'Ricinifolia'	(May—August)
Bougainvillea (many varieties)	(May—August)
Petrea volubilis	(May—August)
Rosa chinensis var. *minima*	(May—September)
Tibouchina semidecandra	(April—September)

7

July and August

This is hot and sunny weather but hardly vacation time for the indoor gardener. If you are growing many cool-room plants, they need special attention now—daily misting, shading at the windows, and a small fan running at low speed to keep air moving. Warmth-preferring plants need almost the same treatment; it is best to keep down the heat in all growing areas. However, a few dog days will not kill plants. Of course, an air conditioner operating at minimum capacity is ideal but not necessary. I have successfully grown hundreds of plants through many steaming summers with few fatalities.

Spray the growing area with a general all-purpose insecticide at least every second week now. If a few ladybugs invade, let them be—they eat insects. Be sure tender plants are shaded from hot sun; Begonias, some Orchids, and certain

ACANTHUS MONTANUS (above)
EPISCIA (below)

other plants develop leaf burn if not protected. Enjoy your flowering plants now: cut the blooms or, if you prefer, place pots directly in the living room or on the dining table for decoration. A morning inspection of the plant room is exciting; there is always something new in flower.

For Warmer Rooms

Acanthus montanus, from tropical Africa, is rarely seen in collections; yet it is an attractive and dependable plant with a tall stalk of pinkish-white flowers surrounded by green bracts. Plants grow well with little sun; a north window is fine. Pot in sandy soil and water heavily except just after flowering, when about a month of dry rest is advisable. *A. mollis*, somewhat larger, is also good, with lilac flowers and big, decorative leaves.

Browallia speciosa major, with blue flowers, is lovely in the window garden. It blooms with little sun, average humidity, and moderate watering. For a glorious display put four or five plants in a 6-inch pot; pinch growing tips occasionally to encourage branching. Seeds planted in February make blooming plants this month. There are other fine species: *B. americana*, with small blue-and-white flowers; and *B. viscosa*, dark blue.

Costus igneus, the Spiral Ginger, from Central and South America, is one of my great favorites. Flowers are 3 inches across, brilliant orange, and ruffled, with a crepe-paper texture. The succulent leaves of this delightful plant form a spiral pattern. Keep soil damp and grow at a west window. Although not the easiest to bring into bloom, it is worthwhile.

Episcia really thrives in summer; plants offer brilliance of flower and foliage. Given proper conditions, Episcias grow all year. Use a mixture of leaf mold, peat moss, and sand for potting, and keep the plants well watered and in the sun these

17
COSTUS IGNEUS

summer months. Although many Episcias are trailing plants, there are bushy species, too. I grow *E. cupreata*, with copper leaves and red flowers; *E. lilacina*, with bronze leaves and blue flowers; and *E. pinkiscia*, with metallic-bronze leaves and pink flowers.

Jatropha pandurifolia, a recent introduction as a house plant, is a great success. My plant blooms continually in summer, and the red clusters are delightful. It grows readily under average home conditions: some sun, about 30 per cent humidity, and copious watering. This one is for lazy gardeners.

Pelargonium crispum variegatum, a popular Geranium, has lavender flowers and lemon-scented, yellow-marked leaves. Grow it in sun and let the soil dry out a little between waterings.

Rechsteineria leucotricha, the Brazilian Edelweiss, is spectacular: four large leaves coated with silky hairs form a leaf rosette from which the red tubular flowers emerge—a colorful, open-faced display. Grow this plant at a sunny window and keep it moist except just after flowering, when a two- to three-week rest is needed.

Zantedeschia Rehmannii, the Pink Calla, is suitable for pot culture and is a lovely addition to the indoor garden. For bloom in summer, start plants in the fall, one bulb to a 6-inch container. Until growth starts, keep shaded and water only moderately. Then place at a sunny window and drench soil frequently. Keep foliage growing for a few months after flowering. Then dry off the bulb and store it in a cool place, in the pot, until next year. Also rewarding is the White Calla, *Z. aethiopica*, and the Yellow Calla, *Z. Elliottiana*.

For Coolest Area (Preferably Air-conditioned)

Coelogyne ochracea is a dainty Orchid with a funny-face

flower that stares at you. It is orange and white—nice summer colors. Flowers are so fragrant that they are worth having for their scent alone. This is a charmer that wants sun, good humidity, and liberal watering. Dry plants out for about a month before and after flowering. Pot in small containers of fir bark (Chapter 13).

Gloriosa Rothschildiana, the Glory-Lily, grows from a tuber and is a joy because two months after potting it produces beautiful orange-crimson, lily-like blooms. You can pot the tubers in commercial packaged soil.

Plumbago capensis, a sturdy, bushy plant, brings cool blue color to the window. A well-grown specimen is covered with clouds of blossoms—quite a sight. It blooms all summer and requires lots of water and feeding. Sunshine is needed for a good crop of flowers, as is also a short winter rest—say three weeks. This is a fine addition to the indoor garden; it can be grown in the same pot for several years.

Zephyranthes, the Rain-Lilies, are small grassy plants with white or yellow or red flowers. Allow four or five bulbs to a 6-inch pot. When plants are in full growth, keep the soil fairly wet. Grow in full sun. When flowers fade, let foliage mature fully. In winter, give plants very little water.

For Basket and Bracket

Achimenes, related to the Gloxinia, has velvety flowers in a rainbow of colors; perhaps red is the most popular. If you grow one of these splendid plants you will want more. They need sun, humidity, and plenty of water to blossom, and they need a short rest after flowering. Clean the soil from the tubers and store them in a paper sack for replanting in spring. Here is summer color for little effort. *A. longiflora* is blue, *A. patens*, red; and there are countless hybrids in various shades.

18

ZANTEDESCHIA

Cobaea scandens, the Cup-and-Saucer Vine, bears violet-and-green flowers. The feathery leaves have tendrils that cling to a trellis. This is a thirsty plant that needs plenty of water and lots of sun to bloom. Grows well warm or cool.

Mandevilla splendens has summery pink flowers with shiny green leaves. It grows easily for me with sun, liberal watering, and an occasional pruning. It is similar to the June-flowering *Dipladenia amoena,* but much larger.

FOR A CHALLENGE

Eucomis punctata (*comosa*), the Pineapple-Lily, produces a regal stalk of small creamy-white flowers. The plant gets its name from the rosette of leaves, which is similar to that formed by the Pineapple plant. Plant the bulbs in late fall, one to a 6-inch pot, and water moderately until April, when growth starts. Then water heavily. For success, grow this one as cool as possible through the summer.

IF YOU HAVE ROOM

Agapanthus, the African-Lily, is a gem. I grow three plants in my unheated pantry (which is almost a greenhouse), and I am always willing to accept more. The prettiest is perhaps *A. africanus,* the Lily-of-the-Nile, with blue flowers. *A. intermedius* also has dark-blue flowers but is a smaller plant, and *A. orientalis* is white. These plants need rich soil and large containers, say 10 inches in diameter. Water them freely now and mist them frequently to lower the heat; they like it cool. In fall and winter keep them somewhat dry.

Epiphyllum, the Orchid Cactus, is beautiful in bloom, unsightly without flowers. I suffer with my plant through winter and spring and by the time I gather courage to discard it in summer, it bursts forth with such magnificent pink-red flowers that I decide to keep it. My plant is one of countless hy-

19

FUCHSIA

brids; there must be about four thousand. If you have a night-blooming variety it is probably *E. oxypetalum*. The flowers of hybrids are red, purple, or white. In winter I keep my plant cool, with only occasional watering, and in summer it grows in a sunny window in the plant room. Flowers last only a few days but even so are worthwhile. In California I have seen smaller hybrids, only 14 inches high, that bloom well. These are highly desirable and are available from mail-order houses in the West.

From the Florist

Fuchsia has been a favorite of gardeners for many years, and with a little extra care the gift plant does well at home. Most Fuchsias are hybrids in red, purple, and white. Grow them as cool as possible now, at a bright but not sunny window, and water them heavily. In mid-autumn let plants rest and water only moderately. In spring, prune and resume watering. Fuchsias are notorious for dropping their buds. I have no remedy to offer for this, but sudden changes of temperature are probably a factor.

Impatiens Sultanii, Patient Lucy, offers a mass of scarlet, rose-pink, or white blossoms throughout the summer. Plants are tolerant of heat but not of sun. They often continue to bloom until October.

Still Colorful

Aeschynanthus speciosus	(June—August)
Clerodendrum Thomsoniae	(May—September)
Dipladenia amoena	(June—July)
Episcia, all varieties	(July—September)
Kaempferia roscoeana	(June—August)
Kohleria, many varieties	(June—August)
Nerium Oleander	(June—September)
Vriesea splendens	(June—October)

CAMPANULA ISOPHYLLA (above)
PENTAS LANCEOLATA (below)

8

September

Aᴜᴛᴜᴍɴ bows in this month and, although the days may still be warm and plants could remain out, the nights are unpredictable. Temperatures in the forties are possible, so by mid-month it is best to bring everything inside—after a thorough insecticide spraying. Keep windows open as much as possible while plants become acclimated to the less pleasing conditions of indoor living. Take inventory; make sure you have all the plants you want for winter bloom. Those that require a winter rest should be separated from active growers. Repot and prune plants that need it.

Fᴏʀ Wᴀʀᴍ Rᴏᴏᴍs (68°-78° F.)

Aechmea fasciata, a robust urn-shaped Bromeliad, now leads the way with a pink brush of tiny blue flowers. Even without bloom the frosty foliage is colorful enough to make this a valued plant. Grow it at a west window with good humidity, some sun, and frequent watering. My plant is potted in osmunda fiber (Chapter 13) and blooms with little extra attention. Like most members of the Pineapple family, it flowers only once and then gradually dies down, but not before producing offshoots for next year. When these are about 3 inches long cut them from the base of the parent plant and pot separately.

Astrophytum Asterias, the autumn-blooming Star Cactus from Mexico, is apple-green, with the look of a sea urchin. Grow it in sandy soil at a window with good light; water moderately all year. This is more apt to bloom indoors than other Cacti, and the flowers are a pretty yellow and red.

Pentas lanceolata, the Egyptian Star-Cluster, is a splendid tropical that grows vigorously and produces wonderful wheels of pink or lavender flowers. Good humidity, some sun, and liberal watering are necessary while plants are in growth. A loose soil mixture is best. Pinch back branches occasionally in summer. You are certain to be delighted with this one.

Rivina humilis, the Rouge Plant, small, delicate, and ornamental with bright red berries, thrives at my window. It takes care of itself and needs nothing more than some sun and water. Highly recommended to the inexperienced window gardener.

For Cool Rooms (52°-68° F.)

Brassavola nodosa, the Lady-of-the-Night, is easily mistaken for a Cactus with thick solitary leaves; but once the lovely flowers open, we see that it is an orchid. Blooms are dramatic. Just one perfumes a room in early evening. Only 14 inches tall, this plant needs heavy watering in summer and fall, less water the rest of the year. With full sun and high humidity, this is an Orchid that really puts on a wonderful show.

Campanula isophylla, one of the fine indoor Bellflowers, starts blooming in August but reaches its peak now. The lavender-blue flowers and gray foliage cascading gracefully over the pot rim are delightful. Plants bloom well with sun, plenty of water, and some feeding. House-plant specialists can supply mature plants. There are other good Bellflowers for window gardens, among them *C. fragilis,* a fine blue but less floriferous, and *C. Elatines* var. *alba plena,* with double white flowers.

For Basket and Bracket

Hoya carnosa, the thick-leaved Wax Plant, is a versatile vine and an ideal house plant. The clusters of white, waxen, quite fragrant bloom are sometimes called "porcelain flowers." Plants will thrive in bright light without sun. In bud, Hoyas need little water, and it is wise not to move them around. Once flowers open, increase the amount of water. Give plants a winter rest and grow them in small pots. Because flowers are borne year after year on the same branches, do not prune these. I have grown the following species with success: *H. bella,* a miniature with white flowers; *H. Keysii,* with pinkish-brown flowers; and *H. motoskei,* white.

For a Challenge

Allophyton mexicanum, the Mexican-Foxglove, is seldom grown; but the lavender clusters that first appear in summer and are now at their peak make this plant worth a try. It requires sun and a warm place. The dark-green, leathery leaves are also pretty and the plant is small, an advantage if you have a large collection.

Schizostylis coccinea, the Rain Lily, adorns a window with scarlet flowers on tall stems. An Iris family member, this blooms only with considerable care. Plant dormant rhizomes in 6-inch pots in late spring in a loose loam mixture. After growth starts, water plants well through flowering and until foliage matures. When leaves die back, store plants dry until next spring.

IF YOU HAVE ROOM

Allamanda cathartica Hendersonii, an evergreen climber, at one time graced my plant room with glorious huge yellow flowers. Unfortunately the plant lived only a short time. After I lost it, I did some research and discovered where my culture was at fault. The plant must be tightly potted; this is important, and so are frequent shifts from one pot size to the next. The minimum suitable temperature is 60° F. and these are greedy plants that need heavy feeding. After flowering they must rest until about November, and in January they must be severely pruned. Two smaller Allamandas that are more suitable for indoors are *A. nerifolia*, with Oleander-like leaves and yellow flowers, and *A. violacea*, with maroon blooms.

Strelitzia Reginae, the popular Bird-of-Paradise flower, possibly has been the cause of more questions than any other tropical. Through the years I have grown seven "birds"—in oil cans, wooden tubs, crocks, and pots. My three successes each had ten to twelve leaves. The theory is that for bloom there must be more than seven leaves, and my experience confirms this. The flower is familiar—orange and blue—its form like that of a bird poised for flight. Foliage is large and plants are 3 to 4 feet tall. They thrive with three hours of sun when planted in rich, sandy soil and alternately watered heavily and dried out severely. If you want this fine but very large flowering plant, start with a mature specimen.

FROM THE FLORIST

Chrysanthemum is gay and colorful now; it is a gift plant that blooms well for some weeks. Moderate watering, good light (but little sun), and fair humidity keep it decorative. Chrysanthemums come in a wide range of attractive colors.

STILL COLORFUL

Achimenes	(July—September)
Agapanthus	(July—September)
Browallia speciosa	(July—September)
Jatropha pandurifolia	(July—September)
Zephyranthes hybrids	(July—September)
Plumbago capensis	(July—October)

21

SOLANDRA GUTTATA (above)
HOLMSKIOLDIA SANGUINEA (below)

9

October

Tʜᴇ trees outside are lovely with color now, but bare winter is not far away. Through the next months we look to the indoor garden to brighten our days. This is the last chance to buy new plants before cold weather makes shipping hazardous. Artificial heat starts now and it is important to check soil frequently; plants dry out faster than we think at this time of year.

Fᴏʀ Wᴀʀᴍ Rᴏᴏᴍs (68°-78° F.)

Beloperone guttata, the Shrimp Plant, is now brilliant with color. The pink-tinged bracts and white flowers somehow do resemble shrimp. This is a fine plant for a bright sunny window, and now it requires nothing more than liberal watering and an occasional misting of foliage. In winter, do not water as much. My plant in a 10-inch pot is a robust specimen; I purposely prune it severely in late summer to keep it bushy. Recently I have seen a yellow shrimp plant advertised, and I am tempted to try it also.

Holmskioldia sanguinea, the Chinese-Hat Plant, in a guise of small flowers brings orange hats to the window. This is a delight and very pretty. Because this oddity is exacting, I keep it with my Orchids in high humidity and full sun. It requires moisture throughout the year.

Lycaste aromatica, the Cinnamon Orchid, is fragrant and pretty, with bright yellow flowers. To make it bloom, rest it without water for a few weeks toward late September. Then after flowering this month, *grow it completely dry for four to six weeks.* Wait until new growth shows in spring before watering again. Once foliage starts to expand, flood the "soil" about twice a week. Pot in fir bark (Chapter 13) and grow in full sun for good flower production; a healthy plant bears six to eight blooms. It is deciduous and foliage fades before, with, or after blooming, so do not be concerned when leaves fall.

Osmanthus fragrans, Sweet-Olive, is satisfactory but not spectacular. It is the scent of the tiny white flowers appearing all winter that makes it attractive. A summer outdoors is almost a necessity. My plant came as a cutting from a friend in Mississippi, and it was difficult to get it started. If you start your own plant, as I did, keep the cutting moist and humid.

For Cool Rooms (52°-68° F.)

Exacum affine, the German-Violet, is covered with charming blue flowers for many weeks. They are fragrant and have bright yellow eyes. A biennial, this requires full sun to bloom heavily. Keep evenly moist, with average humidity.

Punica Granatum var. *nana*, the Dwarf Pomegranate, is an excellent indoor grower, with orange-scarlet flowers and red fruit. Foliage is olive-green, and the plant has a bonsai appearance; it is unique in the indoor garden. Pot this dwarf tree in a shallow container where it appears most decorative. My plant is three years old now and one of my favorites.

For Basket and Bracket

Begonia 'Elsie M. Frey' is a lovely hybrid with exquisite metallic-green, red-lined leaves and pink flowers. Pot in rich soil and keep moderately moist, not soggy. Like most Begonias, it is a most satisfactory, long-blooming house plant and looks charming hanging from a basket.

For a Challenge

Hedychium coronarium is the Ginger-Lily. I especially like this plant and recommend it to anyone who can put it outside in summer. The broad-petaled white flowers swathed in bracts have a sweet perfume and the foliage is lush, green, and graceful. In spring, I keep my plant with the Orchids where there is high humidity and sun. I frequently drench the soil; in summer, I sink the pot in the garden in full sun. When the weather turns cool in late September, I bring it back to a south window; in a few weeks, the graceful white flowers appear. I have seen *H. Gardnerianum*, another attractive Ginger, blooming in conservatories, where its green bracts and red flowers are spectacular. Unfortunately, this one does not respond to home culture.

If You Have Room

Neoregelia carolinae is a lush green Bromeliad with open rosette growth. The tiny violet-colored flowers appear in the cup of the plant when the periphery and lower parts of the straplike leaves turn red—a volcano of fire that remains col-

22

HEDYCHIUM CORONARIUM

orful for nine months. Where else but in the Bromeliad family could you find such an exciting house plant? Mine grows beautifully at a west window, where I keep it fairly wet all year. Wash foliage occasionally to freshen the colorful leaves.

Solandra guttata, the Chalice Vine from Mexico, has enormous, vivid yellow flowers and attractive glossy green leaves. If you can get it to bear even a few flowers, it will be worthwhile. I saw this vine blooming in a large tub on the deck of a California house. My plant is still small. I grow it at a southeastern exposure and am hoping that I can induce it to bloom.

FROM THE FLORIST

Crocus, the autumn-flowering type, is colorful now with purple or yellow flowers; it offers a fine decorative touch for autumn. Plants from the florist stay fresh for several weeks and are charming additions indoors. Just keep them well watered and in bright light.

STILL COLORFUL

Aechmea fasciata	(September—January)
Pentas lanceolata	(September—January)
Brassavola nodosa	(September—October)
Hoya carnosa	(September—October)
Hoya bella	(September—October)
Allamanda cathartica Hendersonii	(August—October)
Strelitzia Reginae	(September—October)

HIBISCUS (above)
ERANTHEMUM NERVOSUM (below)

10

November

As gray skies and snowy days come to the Midwest, the indoor garden is the center of attraction. Many plants require winter sun and should be moved to a south window to get all available light. Others are entering a dormant period and do not need much light; these can be put at north or west windows. Some can be placed under artificial light to compensate for sunless days.

For Warm Rooms (68°-78° F.)

Aechmea calyculata is a dependable Bromeliad with rosettes of dark-green leaves. The cylindrical flower head is brilliant yellow, a honeycomb of color, and it remains vivid until April. My plant at a west window is liberally drenched twice

71

a week all year and is very easy to care for. It is potted in osmunda fiber (Chapter 13).

Begonia dregei, a maple-leaf species, bears white flowers and has bronze leaves with purple veins, red beneath; in all, a lovely plant that blooms quite freely. Grow in partial sunlight with high humidity. Water carefully to keep soil evenly moist but never soaked. There are several varieties of the species available, and most are good.

Ophthalmophyllum Schlecteri, a small stemless succulent, is a curiosity, for it imitates the stones amongst which it grows. Flowers are white or pink and leaves are pale green. Through its growing season, water only moderately; in winter it should have a short dry rest of about four weeks.

Smithiantha cinnabarina, the Temple-Bell Plant, is also sold as *Naegelia.* It is small and adaptable, with red flowers and velvety green foliage. Related to the African-Violets, Smithiantha blooms readily with good moisture, humidity, and some sun. Set each rhizome in a 4-inch pot in spring for bloom this month. After plants flower, store them in a warm place; the winter rest usually lasts three months. *S. zebrina* is also attractive, with yellow-spotted red flowers.

For Cool Rooms (52°-68° F.)

Eranthemum nervosum, sometimes called Blue-Sage, provides a rare color for winter windows. This fine plant needs no rest, so keep it well soaked all year. Occasional pruning and full sun are essential. Plants bloom spectacularly every fall in my plant room and I highly recommend them.

Ruellia Makoyana, a graceful small plant, gives a great deal of pleasure for the little space it occupies. The red, bell-shaped flowers appear among the olive-green, silver-veined leaves which are shaded violet underneath. Place in bright light, rather than in sun, and take care with watering; Ruellia does

24

RUELLIA MAKOYANA

not tolerate dryness, and extreme wetness is also harmful. *R. macrantha* is also desirable; it has larger leaves and rose-colored flowers.

FOR BASKET AND BRACKET

Begonia 'Alleryi' brightens November with arresting blush-pink flowers adorned with silvery hairs and bright-green leaves accented with purple veins. This hybrid is easy to grow but it has one idiosyncrasy—it resents too much water. A good begonia for the inexperienced.

Oncidium ornithorynchum, the Bird's-Head Orchid, is covered with masses of tiny lilac flowers at this time of year. It likes coolness (about 55° F.) but otherwise is undemanding. Drench fir bark well in hot summer weather. Give less water through the cool months after flowering. This fine Orchid forms a flower spike early—in August or September—and it usually takes eight weeks for the first flower to open.

FOR A CHALLENGE

Camellia japonica in bloom is spectacular. If you have adequate space and also considerable patience, do grow it or some of the many varieties. Camellia foliage is green, glossy, and leathery. The beautiful flowers are large and waxlike, red, orange, or white, or variegated pink-and-white or red-and-white. I include these plants here because I know they can be brought to bloom under average home conditions. A friend grows many plants in an unheated (but not freezing) sun porch into which enough warmth comes through the open door of an adjoining room. Here is his advice: Use rich, acid soil with sharp drainage; keep moderately wet (never allow soil to dry out completely); give acid fertilizer at every other watering. Temperature in his sun porch ranges from 42° F. on very cold nights to 70° during the day.

If You Have Room

Hibiscus Rosa-sinensis bears dramatic 5-inch single or double blooms in shades of white, pink, yellow, red, or orange. Although spring and summer flowering is usual, my plant (an unknown variety) buds in November. Each double pink blossom lasts only a day, but at a northwest window, fifty to sixty flowers open over a period of six weeks. I water and fertilize the plant heavily and prune it severely throughout the year—an unorthodox method, I'm sure, but it works. Even small plants bloom freely.

From the Florist

Capsicum annuum, the Pepper Plant, is now a familiar sight at florists' shops. The small red fruits are decorative and last a long time. The plant does well with moderate watering and some sun. Don't try to carry it over. Rather, buy new ones each year, or grow more from seed.

Gardenia jasminoides, an evergreen shrub with scented white flowers, usually blooms this month. These plants are handsome but rather exacting for me. However, I have been successful with this routine: watering, with rain water, spraying foliage daily in hot weather, and fertilizing the plants every other watering. Provide a rich, acid soil and inspect foliage for mealybugs; if they attack, flush them off with water or spray with a nicotine sulfate solution.

Still Colorful

Beloperone guttata	(October—November)
Lycaste aromatica	(October—November)
Neoregelia carolinae	(October—April)
Exacum affine	(October—December)

25

THUNBERGIA ALATA (above)
CALANTHE VESTITA (below)

11

December

THE holiday season gives opportunity to enjoy our flowering plants in the home as table decorations or for color accents in any room. On very cold nights some plants may have to be moved back from windows, or cardboards may be placed in front of the glass to lessen the cold. Artificial heating may be excessive now, so pay attention to your watering schedule. The outdoors is bare in the Midwest, but inside the garden is full of color.

FOR WARM ROOMS (68°-78° F.)

Ardisia crenata welcomes Christmas in my plant room with red berries. This is a handsome plant that flowers in late summer and then produces bright fruit that hangs on for months. Grows best in semi-shade in a small pot of acid soil.

Calanthe vestita, a charming small Orchid, grows from a bulb and, if planted in early spring, bears delicate, scalloped red-and-white flowers this month. The pendent scape is crowded with as many as ten to twelve blossoms. In April, start bulbs in a terrestrial mix (Chapter 13) and water lightly until new growth appears; then soak heavily in summer and keep plants at a sunny window. In September let them dry out to encourage budding; increase moisture as buds form. While plants are in flower, water only once a week; eventually dry off and store, pots and all, in a dark place at 60° F. for replanting next year. It is natural for leaves to fall before plants bloom, so do not be alarmed when this occurs.

Mammillaria Hahniana, a small Cactus, when young blooms with red flowers. Place it at a south window in a small pot of sandy soil and give it little water in winter, quite a lot in summer.

Thunbergia alata, the Black-Eyed-Susan Vine from Africa, seems to make the transition to our indoor gardens with little trouble. You will probably have to start your own plants from seed, but they are delightful. The bell-shaped flowers are creamy yellow, with purple or black centers. Sow seeds in September for bloom this month: sow about five to a 5-inch pot of general-purpose soil; place at a sunny window and water. Other Thunbergias that I have liked are *T. erecta* and *T. grandiflora*, both with blue flowers.

For Cool Rooms (52°-68° F.)

Lobularia maritima, Sweet Alyssum, is a small trailing plant with heads of fragrant white or lavender flowers. It needs good humidity, sunlight, and moderate watering.

Narcissus Tazetta, the Paper-White Narcissus, is worth growing for fragrance alone, but the white flowers are desirable for their appearance, too. Arrange bulbs in bowls of pebbles and water and place them in a cool, dark place for about three weeks, or until growth starts. Then bring them to a cool sunny window. Keep pebbles moist and the water at a level just below the base of the bulbs. *N. orientalis* is also handsome; it has yellow flowers.

FOR BASKET AND BRACKET

Aechmea racinae is a colorful Bromeliad, red, yellow and black, startling in effect. The pendent scape rises from a dark green vase of leaves. A small plant, it is ideal for the window when planted in a 3-inch container of osmunda fiber. Water it moderately all year; it grows well in north light.

Ceropegia Woodii, the Rosary Vine, appears unique with urn-shaped, lavender flowers and dark-green, heart-shaped leaves on trailing stems. Warm air, average humidity, and a winter rest of three weeks keep it in good health. Several plants to a pot make a lovely display. Other attractive possibilities are *C. Barklyii*, with green flowers veined purple and brown, and the white *C. stapeliaeformis*.

FOR A CHALLENGE

Iboza riparia, a shrub with tiny white flowers and broad-toothed leaves, is pretty at this time. Give full sun and plenty of water while it is growing, less moisture the rest of the year. If you carry this over, repot in spring. Difficult but not impossible.

Solanum Pseudo-capsicum, the Jerusalem-Cherry, is a small, dark-leaved shrub with red berries. It needs a bright exposure and—most important—a cool location (55° F. at night). I have never been able to hold over my plant from year to year, but it is possible if you sink the pot in the garden for the summer. I have also seen *S. jasminoides* in bloom at conservatories. It is an attractive climber with fragrant, white flowers.

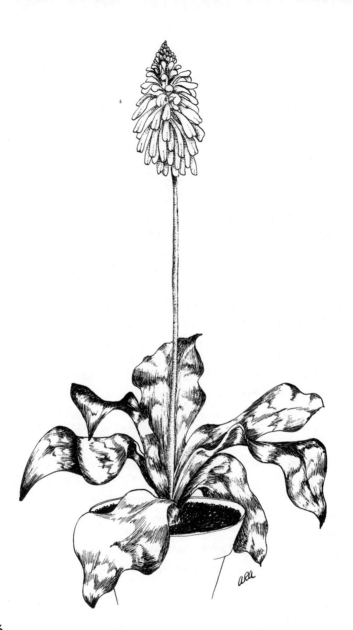

26

VELTHEIMIA VIRIDIFOLIA

If You Have Room

Aglaonema commutatum, the common Chinese Evergreen, bears large bright-green leaves and fine large white "calla-lily" flowers. A durable plant, it will grow under untoward conditions. Mine has bloomed profusely in December for the last five years, one flower following another.

Veltheimia viridifolia, a Lily relative from South Africa with handsome large green leaves, gives a grand show of color with big clusters of twenty to thirty pink flowers. Plants require plenty of water and fertilizer in autumn, and a 3- to 5-week dry rest in summer. Grow at 55° F. in full sun; after flowering, keep plants growing until foliage dies down, then let soil dry out completely. This is a superlative house plant, hard to find but worth the search.

From the Florist

Kalanchoe Blossfeldiana, a very popular miniature and a fine gift plant for this month, bears fiery Christmas-red flowers, and my plant blooms again in April. It requires only a little sun and moderate watering to flower freely. I also grow *K. uniflora*, small and charming, with winter-through-spring pink flowers; *K. Fedtschenkoi*, with blue-green foliage and large clusters of pink flowers at this time; and *K. velutina*, with orange blooms that appear sporadically.

Euphorbia pulcherrima, the familiar Christmas Poinsettia, is probably in your home at this season. This beautiful plant is valued for its red bracts rather than the tiny yellow flowers. To enjoy it for a long time, keep it cool and well watered. If you want to carry it over for another year, dry out the plant after blooms fade and store it at about 50° in a north light until April. Then cut it back to 3 to 4 inches and place it in a sunny window; water lightly, increasing moisture with growth. When it is warm enough outside, put your plant in the sunny garden and fertilize and prune it, allowing only a few strong branches to grow through the summer. When the weather turns cool (about 55° F.) bring the plant to a semi-shady window and increase moisture until buds appear. Successfully carrying over a Poinsettia can be a real satisfaction.

STILL COLORFUL

Aechmea calyculata	(November—March)
Oncidium ornithorynchum	(November—January)
Ruellia Makoyana	(November—January)
Begonia 'Alleryi'	(November—March)

5-LYCASTE AROMATICA, A MEDIUM
  SHOWY ORCHID   *(above)*
6-AN AMENABLE BROMELIAD,
  AECHMEA FASCIATA   *(center)*
7-A SMALL EPIPHYLLUM HYBRID
  WITH LARGE BLOOMS   *(below)*

8-FROM INDIA, CROSSANDRA INFUNDIBULIFORMIS   *(above)*
9-ONE OF THE LOVELY JACOBINIAS   *(below)*

Part II *How to Grow Flowering Plants in the House*

FLOWERING HOUSE PLANTS

FOR A START

Abutilon — Flowering-Maple

Aechmea calyculata
Agapanthus africanus — Lily-of-the-Nile
Billbergia nutans — Queen's Tears
Ceropegia Woodii — Rosary Vine
Clivia miniata — Kafir-Lily
Dendrobium Pierardii
Euphorbia splendens — Crown-of-Thorns
Gloriosa Rothschildiana — Glory-Lily
Hoya carnosa — Wax Plant
Neomarica gracilis — Apostle Plant
Vriesea splendens — Flaming Sword
Zygocactus truncatus — Christmas Cactus

❧§§❧

12

Where to Grow Plants for Health and Display

Any room with windows can be a growing area for plants; there are kinds for every exposure. When possible, keep plants near windows where they will receive natural light; none can grow in profound shade. If your indoor garden must be limited to a window sill, an easy arrangement is to set pots in clay saucers in heavy-duty Fiberglas boxes that are made in various lengths to fit sills. The boxes hold any water that spills over and thus prevent stains on wood. Or you might want to use a layer of pebbles in these containers.

An enclosed, heated sun porch is a good place for plants, and this is my best location. Here it is possible to group plants without crowding, and this makes watering easier. I also have a 20- × 48-inch planter on the living room floor under a bay window; the box contains a layer of gravel chips and the outside metal edge is concealed by a border of bricks, set lengthwise. I do not plant directly in the box but place pots on top of the gravel. Thus I can move them around at will. This is a particularly good set-up for larger plants; there is ample light, and humidity is created by the excess water that evaporates from the chips. It takes only a few minutes to water this whole garden.

For small or medium-sized plants a standard window is a good location; ready-made metal or glass shelves with brackets are easily attached, and four levels will give space for some forty pots with clay saucers or plastic trays under them to catch water. Pedestal tables are often window-sill height and these are excellent for specimen plants. Tables are also good for display in a living-room corner near a window where a decorative accent is attractive.

Bathrooms, too, are fine for plants. The humid warmth and diffused light are beneficial to many tropicals.

What to Select

Flowering plants can be classified according to their temperature requirements: warm, 68° to 78° F.; cool, 52° to 68° F.; and cold (unheated areas, but not freezing), 40° to 52° F. When you select plants, try to have their cultural requirements in mind. Most species prefer either warmth or coolness; only a few require the cold of an almost unheated area. If you have a special room for plants, as I do, you will find that a northwest corner is quite cool, whereas the southeast exposure is warm. There is a radiator at each end of my porch, so it is a simple matter to turn off the heat in winter in the cool section if it gets too warm there.

In my pantry, I grow about thirty plants—those that like it cold. They are placed at a small south window where the winter temperature is about 40° F. at night, 50° by day. This is ideal for species that are resting or for those that naturally grow best where it is cold.

WHEN TO BUY PLANTS

Spring and fall are the best times to acquire new plants. In warm spring weather new arrivals soon make growth, and in early autumn there is time for adjustment before cold weather. I rarely buy in winter. Shipping is risky then and climatic change too drastic. Consider that new purchases have enjoyed greenhouse conditions with high humidity, ample sun, and warmth, so that it takes a few weeks for plants to become acclimated to less perfect home conditions. Keep an eye on them during this time. Some may lose a few leaves, but avoid soaking a plant to hasten the readjustment period. Rather water it sparingly, place it out of direct sun but in warmth and do not fertilize. More new plants are destroyed in the first few weeks at home than at any other time. I had an Amazon-Lily, *Eucharis grandiflora*, that arrived wilted; it took eighteen days for it to recover.

Preferably, buy mature plants; they become acclimated more readily than young ones and are not much more expensive. Seedlings and plants grown from seed are of course a delight, but sometimes they are difficult to start at home. However, in some cases, the only way to have a plant you really want is to grow it from seed. Although I have a propagating box for stock, I also keep a jar filled with water in a shaded place at a kitchen window. Often I snip cuttings and pop them in. If they root, I plant them; if they don't, I discard them.

If you inspect new arrivals for insects, you can avoid trouble before it starts. When I receive an order from a grower I do not know, I isolate his plants for a few days just to make sure there are no pests hidden in the soil. With the new insecticides, greenhouse plants are rarely infested. Years ago this was a problem, not so now.

How to Display Your Plants

I prefer standard clay pots; they are inexpensive, come in all sizes, and to me, a well-scrubbed pot is good looking. If you object to the scrubbing, you may be able to buy the new clay pots that are chemically treated to stay clean for months. There are also various decorative containers; these are expensive but excellent to use if you want a pot plant to serve as a decoration. Plastic pots are lightweight and easier to handle and ship than clay containers. This is an advantage if you buy many plants because growers send them already potted, thus saving the shock of immediate transplanting. Plants in plastic pots also require less watering.

Vines and trailers like Hoyas and Columneas look best in hanging baskets or bracket-and-pot units. The brackets attach to walls and the arm, or pot holder, swivels out so a plant can be placed at any angle. Some baskets hang from the ceiling on heavy chains, and many are colorful and handsome but few are inexpensive. The first hanging baskets I bought cost fifty cents each. They were made of wire, and I lined them with sheet moss. A saucer had to be placed on the floor below to catch dripping water, a not too attractive arrangement. Even so, I still prefer these wire baskets because they allow air to circulate around and through the growing medium.

For hanging plants at window-sill level there is a clever pot clip that attaches to the wall directly below the sill and holds the rim of the pot. This is a fine way to grow plants where they can receive maximum light without the need of table or tray. However, a container must be set underneath to catch excess water.

Wrought-iron plant stands are attractive; these hold about ten pots, and the arms are staggered so that water doesn't drip from a plant above onto a plant below. But again, some device for catching water that leaks from the pots must be used.

Inexpensive wire racks are fine for displaying plants, but do not overburden them: they are somewhat lightweight and can easily tip over. And don't overlook a pebble-filled tray on top of a radiator, an excellent location for plants. The heat dries off accumulated water in the pan, thus creating humidity, and the warmth is good for certain species. I place a brick under each end to provide air space below the tray. Then there is no danger of staining the radiator top.

Glass shelves at windows are handsome. These have the advantage of not obstructing light. Metal brackets can be bought packaged with the glass or, if you care to save a little money, you can buy brackets and glass separately at a hardware store.

Actually, any receptacle can be used for plants, from bird cages to wooden tubs to tea pots (lids lost), if sufficient drainage is provided. I have plants in unglazed stone crocks, and these are wonderful because the walls absorb surplus water and evaporation is gradual; a drainage hole is not needed. I rarely throw away any container, because I know I'll eventually use it as a pot.

"FLOWER" ARRANGEMENTS WITH HOUSE PLANTS

After blooming, many house plants rest; some drop leaves, others need to be pruned. When you do this, you can use leaves and branches for decorative arrangements. A few pieces of Ixora foliage and some Bromeliad leaves in a decorative dish with water create a simple but pleasing piece. A cluster of Clerodendrum leaves with a sprig of Pussy-Willow in a tall vase makes another attractive grouping. Snip branches of Spider Plants and arrange them in a shallow bowl of water with some interesting small stones, and you have an Oriental accent for the dining table. Cut a few sprays from a large Asparagus-Fern and add some leathery Bromeliad leaves for an airy composition. Leaves growing on a plant are not always so easily appreciated as one cluster in a beautiful vase.

In making these arrangements, combine contrasting leaf textures and color with solid-mass round leaves and spindly foliage. You will be surprised, as I was, at the compositions you can create; all are easy to make, cost nothing, and add beauty to your home. Try some.

13

Culture of Plants Indoors

A PLANT draws nourishment from soil through the root system, which is limited by the size of the pot. For this reason, it is important that the soil contain adequate nutrients and also that plants be potted properly. A good soil mixture includes loam, leaf mold, peat moss, and sand. Some plants, like Clivia and Strelitzia, thrive with manure in the soil; others require bone meal. Some like Cacti and succulents need more sand than others, while Begonias require considerable humus. I do not have the time nor the space in my plant room (and neither do most indoor gardeners) to mix soil, so I buy it by the bushel from a local greenhouse and add various materials for the plants that require something special. Packaged soil is good, too, but somewhat expensive if a great deal is required.

A new mixture known as Peat-Lite, developed at Cornell

FLOWERING PLANTS FOR EVERY WINDOW

SOUTH

Abutilon *species & hybrids*
Achimenes *species & hybrids*
Allamanda nerifolia
Bougainvillea *hybrids*
Browallia speciosa
Campanula isophylla
Ceropegia Woodii
Citrus *plants*

Cobaea scandens
Episcia *species & hybrids*
Euphorbia splendens
Haemanthus Katharinae
Ixora *hybrids*
Kalanchoe Blossfeldiana
Nerium Oleander
Thunbergia *species*

EAST AND WEST

Aechmea calyculata
Agapanthus africanus
Anthurium Scherzerianum
Begonia 'Alleryi'
Beloperone guttata
Columnea *hybrids*
Eranthemum nervosum

Exacum affine
Guzmania monostachia
Jacobinia carnea
Manettia bicolor
Neomarica gracilis
Passiflora alato-caerulea
Plumbago capensis

NORTH

Aechmea racinae
Aeschynanthus *species*
Aglaonema commutatum
Aphelandra *species*
Begonia 'Elsie M. Frey'
Billbergia nutans
Calceolaria

Chlorophytum elatum
Clivia miniata
Hoya carnosa
Neoregelia carolinae
Oxalis *species & hybrids*
Ruellia Makoyana

University, is now being tried out. It contains vermiculite, peat moss, superphosphate, and ground dolomitic limestone. I have not used this, but the published results are encouraging.

Orchids and Bromeliads are mostly epiphytic (i.e., they are air plants and derive the moisture for their development chiefly from the air) and should be potted in osmunda fiber or fir bark. Osmunda fiber is sold in large chunks and must be soaked in water the night before it is used; it is then easy to work with. Buy medium-grade fir bark. Although growers advocate soaking this material, too, I use it dry without any difficulty. After they are potted, soak plants well. The Orchids and Bromeliads that require a terrestrial mix grow in standard house-plant soil. (I indicate plant preferences in the individual descriptions in Part I.)

If you buy plants from a local greenhouse, try to have them repotted there, for they are usually pot-bound. Repotting beforehand saves time, and you know then that you have a freshly potted plant.

ABOUT POTTING

It is important that plants be potted properly; this one simple procedure can make the difference between success and failure. Provide good drainage: water will be applied repeatedly to the same soil mass and, if the soil is packed and becomes waterlogged because water cannot drain off, plants are doomed. But plants should not be loosely potted either; roots must be in firm contact with soil so as to absorb nutrients.

Scrub pots and shards (broken pieces of pots for drainage layer) clean before repotting. Size of pot, of course, depends upon size of plant. Except in the rare cases mentioned, do not put a small plant into a big pot; this is asking for trouble.

The damp unused soil hampers root growth and a sour condition usually develops.

Good potting or repotting, as the case may be, comes with experience. Here is the way I pot a plant: I fit a layer of shards over and around the drainage hole, along with a few bits of charcoal. Then I sprinkle a thin layer of soil over the shards in the bottom of the pot, set the plant in the center, and fill in around it with soil, pressing soil firmly but not packing it. Repeating this procedure, I fill the pot to within an inch of the rim but no higher, or watering will be difficult. Next, I water heavily and label and stake the plant as necessary. It is then placed in a warm, semi-shaded spot for a few days.

When I am repotting, I shake and pry off as much old soil as possible from a root ball before resetting a plant in another (and usually larger) pot.

The Importance of Light

Plants need light; some require less than others, but none can grow for any length of time in heavy shade. A chart at the end of this book specifies individual light requirements.

As the seasons change so does the intensity of light, and this must be given consideration. In winter, days are short, the sun is low in the sky, and light is weak. In summer, light is powerful, and some shading is almost always needed at the windows. I find a window screen gives enough shade for my plants, but a thin curtain may be necessary for yours. In general, south and east windows offer the best light; however, a west exposure is adequate for many plants, and some species grow well at a north window.

Day length is also important in bringing indoor plants into bloom. Some, like the Christmas Cactus and many Orchids, flower when days are short. Others, like Plumbago, need long days.

With Artificial Light

Fluorescent lights open exciting new possibilities to indoor gardeners. Room dividers, closets, basement areas, and other unused spaces are now being used for plants. Not all kinds respond to artificial light, but a great many do. Growing plants "under lights" is still rather new, and there is much to be learned, of course. The intensity and duration of home-made "sunshine" are important aspects of this new technique, and these must be studied. Success with this method also depends on generally good culture.

For the last two years, I have grown plants under artificial light in a metal planter stand with brackets and canopy. I use two 40-watt daylight fluorescent tubes and two 15-watt incandescent bulbs. One tray is for long-day plants, so the timer is set to provide light for 15 hours; the short-day plants in another tray get 13 hours. The light tubes are set 3 inches above the *tops* of the leaves, and the canopy with the fluorescent lights is raised as the foliage grows taller.

For me, the Gesneriads and Begonias grow rapidly, but bloom production seems about the same as for plants at the window. The advantage in artificial light is that I can put my rare and favorite species under the "sun" during cloudy winter days. In this way, artificial light has been a boon, and many plants thrive that otherwise might have failed because of lack of light.

This is a brief summary of how I use artificial light; it is by no means conclusive. For detailed information I highly recommend *Fluorescent Light Gardening* by Elaine C. Cherry, (D. Van Nostrand Co., Inc., Princeton, N.J., 1965).

Humidity Requirements

Although such plants as Kalanchoe and *Euphorbia splendens* grow well indoors in a dry atmosphere, there are many others, too pretty to miss, like Columnea and Achimenes, that require humid conditions. Space humidifiers are the answer; they are inexpensive now, and moisture in the air is not only beneficial to plants, but to us as well. If you are without a humidifier and want to grow tropicals, you must mist the growing area *at least once a day*.

Metal planters or trays with gravel and water in the base offer some humidity, but they can produce only a small percentage of what is required. Growing many plants together in one area also helps to create humidity, but hardly enough. Humidity can be measured by an inexpensive hygrometer, an instrument that looks like a thermometer. Some instruments conveniently include both hygrometer and thermometer.

VENTILATION

In addition to light and humidity there must be adequate ventilation, too. Few plants, if any, survive a stuffy atmosphere. Whenever possible, do allow fresh air to enter the growing area, *but avoid direct drafts on the plants*.

WATERING

I believe that indoor plants should be watered heavily to grow. My plants are drenched in their growing seasons, which for most are spring and summer. And when weather is extremely hot in July and August, I water the larger specimens twice a day. However, I always make sure by evening that pots are not standing in saucers of water. In autumn and winter, too, except for those that are resting, I keep my plants reasonably wet; artificial heat dries out soil faster than you may realize.

I cannot advise exactly when to water or how much. It depends on general conditions. Pot size must be considered;

small containers dry out fast, large ones, slowly. In a sunny south window, drying is faster than at a northern exposure. A perfect balance of light, humidity, temperature, and water is ideal but seldom attained with plants in the home. The best you can do is to consider all conditions and decide on your own watering schedule. Observe and experiment. In time, you can determine when a plant needs water and about how much. At first, follow the general rule: Soak thoroughly and then let soil dry out before watering again. Like most things, indoor gardening takes practice.

Foliage needs washing at least once a month, more often in the city, to keep breathing pores from clogging. A weekly shower in the tub or sink keeps plants healthy and fresh looking.

FERTILIZING

In nature, roots can spread out to absorb more and more nutrients from the soil, but indoor plants confined to a pot cannot do this. Eventually soil is depleted and plants must be fed. I use a general 10-10-5 soluble fertilizer (composed of 10 parts of nitrogen to 10 parts of phosphorus and 5 parts of potash). While plants are growing I feed them every other watering, except in winter. About once a month is sufficient then. Don't feed very young plants, or those newly potted, or those that are resting.

How PLANTS REST

When I discuss plants with friends or lecture at garden clubs, I have a great deal to say about resting plants. This seems to some to be a mystery. However, a plant is a living organism and, like people who sleep to regain energy, plants at some time of the year need a rest period. From my experience with Orchids I discovered that a resting time is vital because many species come from climates with sharply de-

A FEW GENERAL SUGGESTIONS

Culture for individual plants is given in Part I. Here are a few suggestions to help you avoid the more common problems.

• Be sure plant is potted in appropriate sized container with provision for drainage. Avoid wet, hard-packed soil.

• All plants need light. See charts for individual requirements.

• Try to maintain a difference of no more than 10° F. to 15° F. between day and night temperatures. As in nature, cooler nights are healthful. *Avoid drafts and contact with cold windows.*

• Avoid applying very cold water; use warm water or fill pitcher and allow to come to room temperature before using.

• Water preferably in the morning.

• Through spring and summer, or any period of growth, water heavily; in autumn and winter, water less.

• Spray or wash foliage with water at least once a month to keep plants clean and free of pests.

• Rain water, or water free of chemicals, is beneficial to plants; whenever possible, use it.

• Feed plants every other watering when in active growth; once a month in winter.

❧❧

fined seasons. There may be torrential rains for months and then weeks of complete dryness. Native conditions more or less determine cycles of growth. Orchids come from all over the world and other flowering house plants do, too.

In general, most of my plants are watered less at some time of the year, usually immediately after flowering, unless this is a time of heavy leaf growth (as with Clerodendrum and Pentas). Some, like Veltheima and Lycaste Orchids, need a long rest, four to six weeks; others, like certain Bromeliads, require only a short sleep, two to three weeks. During these periods I do not water the soil but I do occasionally mist foliage. It is difficult not to water a plant when I see the soil bone dry, but I have found from experience that these resting times are necessary to health. Usually, when it is time to start watering again, the plant itself indicates the need; a green shoot or an eye of growth develops. Of course, there are exceptions and some plants, like Eranthemum, must be kept fairly moist all year, as suggested in the individual plant descriptions.

To Increase Your Plants

When you grow flowering house plants, you are proud of your collection and usually have some that are fairly uncommon, many that are special favorites. These are the ones you will want to multiply, to share with your friends or to increase your own stock.

Propagating plants is exciting, but it is exacting and usually involves a considerable lapse of time before the results are realized. Should you want to go more deeply into the subject, there are many good books on the market that discuss the various methods of plant propagation in detail. If you want to increase your plants just for fun, as I do, here are some of the methods I follow.

Mostly I propagate from stem and leaf cuttings, but occasionally I plant seeds if I want a hard-to-find plant I cannot get any other way. As a rooting medium for cuttings, I like pure sand, although perlite is good, too. Either material encourages root development. I use a large aquarium covered with a glass pane as a propagating case and place this on a radiator at the north window of my plant room. Heat ranges from 68° F. at night to 78° F. through the day; humidity varies from 70 to 80 per cent inside the case. I raise the glass cover occasionally to permit circulation of air. If the glass clouds with moisture, I wipe it off and allow a longer period of ventilation.

For stem cuttings, I snip a 3 to 5 inch cutting from the tip growth with a sharp pocket knife that has been sterilized by holding it a few seconds over a match flame. I usually select cuttings from sturdy stems or branches; base cuttings are fine, too. With a pencil, I make an opening 1 inch deep in the sand, insert the cutting the full inch, and pack the sand around it. I water the cutting well and keep it moist and warm. It takes a few weeks for some cuttings to root, months for others.

In any case, cuttings take time. To find out if they have rooted, pull just one shoot. If the roots are about an inch long, it is time to take up the plants from the sand and put them in separate small pots of soil appropriate to the species. Keep young plants warm and semi-shaded for about a week. Then transfer them to a permanent place in the growing area. For a few more weeks the small plants may need a little pampering.

I tried propagating leaf cuttings because I wanted Rex Begonias. Many kinds are hard to find in local greenhouses and rather than have them shipped, I took leaves, with about an inch of stem attached, from a friend's plants. After cutting across the leaf veins in several places on the under side with a razor blade, I place leaves, right side up, flat on the sand in the cutting box, the stem inserted in the sand. I put small stones on the leaves as weights; it is important to keep them in contact with the sand. Plantlets soon appear along the cuts; they draw nourishment from the old leaf. When the new plants are large enough to handle, cut them apart from the parent leaf and pot them separately. Take leaf cuttings in spring and summer, when plants are usually in active growth. Autumn and winter cuttings are not so reliable.

I am very fond of the Pouch Flower, *Calceolaria*, and the Cup-and-Saucer Vine, *Cobaea scandens*. Sometimes these plants are not available in my area and yet they are too good to miss, so I sow seed. It is a thrill to see your own plants grow from seed, especially when they start to bloom.

Sow seeds from February to April. I usually soak the seeds of these two plants for a few hours to soften their casings. Then I put them in a shallow 4-inch pot of sphagnum moss. I place a 3-inch saucer underneath and a glass dome above, the edges resting on a pencil. (This is a device to provide space for air to circulate.) Keep the moss moist but not wet and give the plantings enough light.

Very fine seeds need not be covered; just scatter them on the sphagnum. Larger seeds should be slightly imbedded. To avoid washing seeds away when you water (some seeds are microscopic), water from the bottom. Warmth, about 72° F. to 80° F., is essential. When seedlings appear, I remove the glass dome. Then I transfer the young plants to small separate pots and put these in a growing area with other plants.

Some flowering house plants, such as Begonias and various succulents, develop crowns. When these get to be mature specimens, it is possible to get new plants from an old one by division, preferably just after the plant has flowered. Remove it from the pot and gently pull the crowns apart; if necessary, cut them apart with a razor blade. Then set each rooted crown in a small pot of appropriate soil. Shade the divisions and water sparingly for a few weeks until more roots have formed.

Some Bromeliads, Orchids and certain other plants produce offshoots, or suckers, at the base. These can be cut off with a sharp sterilized knife and separately potted when they are 3 to 4 inches long. This is an easy way to increase your stock.

Plants like Chlorophytum produce runners that will root if cut off and placed in contact with damp soil. Fill a 3- to 4-inch pot with a mixture of loam, leaf mold and sand, and insert the runner into the center of the pot; it will soon root.

These are the simpler basic ways of increasing your plants. Try them to know the satisfaction of having plants you have really grown yourself.

TROUBLES AND THEIR CAUSES

When plants do not grow well, there is bound to be something wrong. Here are some signs of trouble:

A plant wilts or develops only spindly growth. Very likely light or temperature is not to its liking.

Foliage suddenly withers. This is probably due to a drastic temperature change or a cold draft directly on the plant. Watering with very cold water causes this too.

Dry areas appear on leaves. These are usually caused by impurities in the air—gasoline or industrial fumes.

Burnt or scorched leaf spots occur. These may be caused by direct sunlight magnified through a defect in the window glass. Root damage also causes brown foliage spots.

Buds fail to open. This is an indication of too much sun or, more likely, a too-dry atmosphere. A mist of water may soften the casings and allow buds to open. The need of higher humidity is indicated particularly if buds drop.

PEST AND DISEASE CONTROL

When you get sick, you call a doctor; when plants are afflicted, you must be the doctor. A house plant that is clean and grown under proper conditions is rarely troubled by pests or diseases because, for the most part, it is vigorous enough to resist intruders and ward off disease. Vigilance on your part helps—keeping leaves washed, inspecting plants for early infestations, and regular preventative spraying with a house-plant bomb, usually about once a month. If your plants are seriously attacked, you may need to give them specific treatment—or discard them.

Systemics—insecticides applied to soil—are the latest in pest control. They are available in granular form. Spread material over the soil. Work it in and water well. Roots then draw it into the system or sap stream, which is then toxic. Sucking insects and most chewing insects die when they feed on the juices. The control lasts up to six weeks or longer.

Thrips, small, dark-winged insects, feed on plant juices; they leave thin, papery scars. An aerosol pesticide with malathion eliminates them.

White flies, tiny insects that cluster on the undersides of leaves, are especially fond of Begonias and scented Geraniums. Malathion is the best cure.

Scales, rounded hard- or soft-shelled insects, attach themselves to stems and leaves and are very difficult to get rid of. Their work is easily seen in the general decay of the area they attack. If the infestation is mild, I usually get them off with toothpick or fingernail. If they have a strong foothold, I spray with a nicotine-sulfate solution (Black Leaf 40).

Mealybugs, cottony insects that move slowly all over the plant, cause extensive damage once they get started. Soapy water or a nicotine-sulfate solution applied every third day with a cotton swab helps. If this does not clean up the infestation, a malathion spray will probably get rid of them.

Red spiders (spider mites), demons that cannot be seen, suck sap from leaves and cause gray, brittle areas to develop. I first wash the plants several times in a week; if this does not work, I spray with Dimite, one of the miticides, which is effective against red spider.

Slugs, ugly creatures, rarely invade house plants; they have too much work to tend to in the garden. However, you might find one brought in with potting soil or already in the soil of a plant. Slugs feed at night. An old-fashioned remedy consists of putting out a piece of peeled potato to attract them. They are then easy to dispose of. Or use Slug-it, available in powder form.

Plant lice or aphids, usually black or green, cluster on new growth and deform foliage. Malathion is an effective control.

Springtails, unseen, invade the soil and often appear in saucers after a heavy watering. They do no damage but are a nuisance and easily eliminated with a chlordane or malathion spray.

Nematodes attack roots, cause dwarfed or stunted growth. If nematodes get to a plant your only recourse is to destroy it by burning. Nematodes can cause extensive damage to a collection and are almost impossible to eradicate.

Fungus disease on house plants is rare and I do not try to cope with it; I unhappily but wisely dispose of an affected plant before it has a chance to infect others.

If you are growing many plants indoors, spray them with a pesticide once a month in summer and once every second month the rest of the year. Malathion takes care of most pests, and you can depend on it. I also keep an aerosol pesticide on hand. It saves the trouble of making a solution. Carefully follow the manufacturer's directions when using insecticides and keep them out of reach of children and pets.

14

Summering Plants Outdoors

A SUMMER outdoors is beneficial to most flowering house plants. Sun, refreshing rain, and natural air currents encourage growth and promote fall and winter bloom. Plants get a reserve of strength from a summer outside, particularly if they have to cope with an unusually dull winter. However, some kinds, like Clivia and most Gesneriads, are safer in the house; their foliage may easily be damaged outdoors by strong winds. Other plants, like Plumbago, Heliconia, and Ginger-Lily (*Hedychium*), revel in outdoor conditions.

Many apartments and most houses have a back porch, and this is ideal for plants in summer. Here there is sun but also protection from the noon rays that burn foliage. The roof of the porch (sometimes the floor above) almost creates a lath-house situation.

Set plants on inverted pots (to ward off insect invasion) and place them next to the porch railing, where they can benefit from rain but still be supported. I anchor them with strings to the wooden posts for protection against wind. Outdoors, where evaporation is high, it is important to water heavily; drench the soil in July and August, and feed plants regularly. In the Midwest it is usually safe to put plants outside at the end of May and wise to bring them back to the house soon after Labor Day. However, some flowering species, like the Christmas Cactus and many Orchids, thrive in cool weather and can be left out until October if frost does not threaten.

The garden is another area where plants can have a summer vacation. Select a place under a deep-rooted tree; filtered sunlight coming through leaves is beneficial. Only Cacti, succulents, and some Orchids and Bromeliads require full summer sun. Leave plants in their pots and sink these up to the rim in a garden bed. This conserves moisture. I spread an inch or so of stone over the bottom of each hole to keep roots from growing through drainage holes into the soil. Even so, every few weeks I lift pots to make sure roots are not straying and I turn plants to promote even growth. Hoyas, Oleanders, and Thunbergias are only a few of the many plants that can be summered to advantage in the garden.

A patio is a fine place for larger tub specimens; these look most decorative there, especially the colorful Bromeliads and lush tropicals. Pots can be placed directly on the floor or set into architectural redwood containers, cleverly detailed. Some are octagonal, others square, rectangular, hexagonal, or triangular. Clay and concrete pots are available, too; forms range from kidney shapes to giant urns for some very special plant. Plastic containers are reasonably priced and are usually facsimiles of the clay or stone types.

Because of the short summers in the Midwest I do not plant directly in decorative pots, but spread a thick layer of stones or gravel over the bottom and place the potted plant inside. A covering of sphagnum moss over the pot is added to hold moisture and conceal the pot rim. Then it is easy to bring the plant back to the house when the weather gets cool. Water patio plants heavily unless there is considerable rainfall.

Appendix

Plant Societies

The following Societies publish bulletins or magazines; some are monthlies, others quarterlies. Subscriptions are included in Society memberships. Publications are not available at newsstands.

American Begonia Society
1510 Kimberly Avenue
Anaheim, California

American Camellia Society
Box 2398 University Station
Gainesville, Florida

American Gesneriad Society
109 Copeland Lane
Irvington, California

American Gloxinea Society
220 West Sunset Road
San Antonio 9, Texas

American Orchid Society
Botanical Museum of Harvard University
Cambridge 38, Massachusetts

The Bromeliad Society
1811 Edgecliff Drive
Los Angeles, California

Cactus and Succulent Society of America
820 West 115 Street
Los Angeles, California

Epiphyllum Society of America
500 Grove Place
Glendale 6, California

International Geranium Society
1413 Bluff Drive
Santa Barbara, California

Where to Buy Plants and Supplies

Alberts & Merkel Bros., Inc.
P.O. Box 537
Boynton Beach, Fla.

Color catalog, 50 cents.
Wide selection of flowering
plants.

Antonelli Bros.
2545 Capitola Rd.
Santa Cruz, Calif.

Begonias, Gesneriads.

Barrington Greenhouses
860 Clements Bridge Rd.
Barrington, N.J.

Flowering plants, Begonias.

California Jungle Gardens
11977 San Vicente Blvd.
Los Angeles, Calif.

Tropical plants; Bromeliads.
Listings available.

Fantastic Gardens
9550 SW 67th Ave.
Miami, Fla.

Unusual plants; Orchids and
Bromeliads.

House Plant Corner
P.O. Box 810
Oxford, Md.

Supplies.

Johnson Cactus Gardens
Paramount, Calif.

Fine selection of Cacti, succulents. Catalog.

Logee's Greenhouses
55 North St.
Danielson, Conn.

Excellent catalog. Many
hard-to-find plants.

Merry Gardens Camden, Maine	Catalog 25 cents. Wide choice of flowering plants.
Oakhurst Gardens P.O. Box 444 Arcadia, Calif.	Unusual bulbs, flowering plants. Orchids and Bromeliads. Catalog 35 cents.
Julius Roehrs Rutherford, N.J.	Catalog. Good selection of all kinds of plants.
Tinari Greenhouses Bethayres, Pa.	Episcias, other Gesneriads.
Tropical Paradise Greenhouses 8825 W. 79th St. Overland Park, Kansas	Catalog 50 cents. Fine selec- tion of flowering plants.

Quick Reference Chart
of Flowering House Plants

SIZE	SUMMER OUTDOORS	EXPOSURE
S (small): to 24 inches	*On porch or in garden	S (sun): 3 to 4 hrs.
M (medium): 24 to 36 inches	for best results	L (bright light): 2 to 3 hrs.
L (large): 36 inches and over		Sh (semishade): 1 to 2 hrs
V vine		

TIME OF BLOOM: Months Indicated

Plant	Size	Time of Bloom	Summer Outdoors	Exposure	Remarks
Abutilon	M	March-June	*	S	Start new plants yearly
Acacia armata	M	March		S	Grow cold (45° F.)
A. Baileyana	M	March		S	Large puffs of flowers
Acalypha hispida	S	May		S	Temporary plant
Acanthus mollis	L	July-Aug	*	L	Good house plants
A. montanus	L	July-Aug	*	L	From tropical Africa
Achimenes longiflora	V	July-Sept		L	Sow seed each year
A. patens	V	July-Sept		L	Sow seed
Aechmea angustifolia	M	Feb-May	*	L	Blue berries
A. calyculata	M	Nov-March	*	Sh	Pot offshoots when 3 in. high
A. chantinii	L	March-June	*	L	Perhaps the best
A. fasciata	M	Sept-Jan	*	Sh	Stays colorful for 6 months
A. fulgens *var.* discolor	L	Feb-April	*	L	Colorful foliage
A. racinae	S	Dec-Feb	*	Sh	Christmas flowering
Aeschynanthus specious	V	June-Aug		L	Keep pot bound
Agapanthus africanus	M	July-Sept	*	L	Keep pot bound
A. intermedius	M	July-Sept	*	L	Keep pot bound
A. orientalis	M	July-Sept	*	L	Keep pot bound
Aglaonema commutatum	M	Dec		Sh	Avoid repotting; top-dress
Allamanda cathartica Hendersonii	L	Aug-Oct	*	S	Prune in spring
A. nerifolia	M	June-Sept	*	S	From Brazil
A. violacea	V	June-Sept.		S	From Brazil
Allium neapolitanum	L	Jan	*	S	Novelty; grows from bulb
Allophyton mexicanum	S	Sept	*	S	Worth a try
Alstroemeria pulchella	M	June	*	S	Rest somewhat in winter

QUICK REFERENCE CHART OF FLOWERING HOUSE PLANTS (Cont.)

SIZE		SUMMER OUTDOORS	EXPOSURE	
S (small):	to 24 inches	* On porch or in garden	S (sun):	3 to 4 hrs.
M (medium):	24 to 36 inches	for best results	L (bright light):	2 to 3 hrs.
L (large):	36 inches and over		Sh (semishade):	1 to 2 hrs.
V	vine			

TIME OF BLOOM: Months Indicated

Plant	Size	Time of Bloom	Summer Outdoors	Exposure	Remarks
Anthurium Scherzerianum	S	Jan-April		Sh	Grow warm with humidity
Aphelandra aurantiaca Roezlii	S	June		L	Needs good air circulation
A. chamissoniana	S	April-May		L	Needs good air circulation
A. squarrosa Louisae	M	April-Sept		L	Needs good air circulation
Ardisia crenata	M	Dec		Sh	Grow cool
Aristolochia elegans	V	April		L	Prune in spring
Arthropodium cirrhatum	M	Feb		S	Grow cool, with humidity
Asparagus Sprengeri	L	Jan		Sh	Spray foliage with water frequently
Astrophytum Asterias	S	Sept		S	Keep somewhat dry in winter
Azalea	M	Jan-April	*	L	Grow cool. Many varieties
Begonia 'Alleryi'	S	Nov-March		L	Easy to grow
B. 'Bow-Arriola'	S	Jan		L	Grow quite dry
B. x cheimantha	S	Jan		L	Many varieties. Grow cool
B. coccinea	S	March-June		L	Angel-wing type
B. dregei	S	Nov		Sh	Grow warm and humid
B. 'Elsie M. Frey'	V	Oct		L	Basket type
B. 'Limminghei'	V	Jan-May		L	Grow warm
B. 'Ricinifolia'	M	May-Aug		L	Robust plant
Beloperone guttata	M	Oct-Nov	*	L	Prune in spring
Billbergia nutans	L	Jan	*	S	Grow as specimen
Bougainvillea	V	May-Aug		S	Many colorful forms
Brassavola nodosa	S	Sept-Oct		S	Dry out in August
Browallia speciosa major	M	July-Sept	*	L	Grow from seed yearly
Calanthe vestita	S	Nov-Feb		L	Dry out severely in November
Calceolaria	S	March	*	L	Temporary house plant
Camellia japonica	L	Nov-March		L	To set buds, grow cold (45°F.)
Campanula isophylla	S	Sept	*	L	Large flowers
C. Elatines *var*. alba plena	M	June-Sept	*	L	Double white flowers
C. fragilis	S	June-Sept	*	L	Another good campanula
Capsicum annuum	S	Nov		S	The Pepper Plant

QUICK REFERENCE CHART OF FLOWERING
HOUSE PLANTS (Cont.)

SIZE	SUMMER OUTDOORS	EXPOSURE
S (small): to 24 inches	* On porch or in garden	S (sun): 3 to 4 hrs.
M (medium): 24 to 36 inches	for best results	L (bright light): 2 to 3 hrs.
L (large): 36 inches and over		Sh (semishade): 1 to 2 hrs.
V vine		

TIME OF BLOOM: Months Indicated

Plant	Size	Time of Bloom	Summer Outdoors	Exposure	Remarks
Ceropegia Barklyii	V			L	Somewhat difficult
C. stapeliaeformis	V			L	Funnel-like flowers
C. Woodii	V	Dec		L	Keep on dry side
Chlorophytum elatum	L	Jan		Sh	Stands abuse
Chorizema cordatum	S	March		S	Cool nights required
Chrysanthemum	M	Sept-Oct	*	L	Gift plant
Cineraria (Senecio cruentus)	M	April		L	Gift plant
Citrus taitensis	L	March	*	S	Lush green foliage
Clerodendrum Bungei	L	June-Sept		L	Somewhat difficult
C. fragrans	L	June-Sept		L	Fragrant
C. Thompsoniae	L	June		L	Best of group
Clivia miniata	L	April		Sh	Grow quite dry for bloom
Cobaea scandens	V	July-Aug	*	S	Sow seeds on edge
Coelogyne cristata	S	Feb		L	Grow cool in November
C. ochracea	S	July-Aug		S	Dry out in April
Columnea arguta	V	April-July		L	Keep in small pots
C. hirta	V	April-July		L	Keep in small pots
C. microphylla	V	April-July		L	Keep in small pots
C. tulae 'Flava'	V	April-July		L	Excellent variety
Costus igneus	S	July-Aug		L	A real beauty
Crassula triebnerii	S	May		S	Rest in winter
Crocus	S	Oct		L	Good indoor decoration
Crossandra infundibuli-formis	M	April-Aug		L	Requires good air circulation
Cyanotis somaliensis	S	May	*	L	Fine house plant
Cyclamen	M	Feb		L	Grow very cool
Cytisus canariensis	S	March	*	S	Cool airy location
Daphne odora	M	Feb		Sh	Avoid overwatering
D. odora marginata	M	Feb-March		Sh	Variegated foliage
Dendrobium densiflorum	L	May	*	L	Fine house orchid
D. Pierardii	S	April-May	*	L	Dry out in February
Dietes bicolor	M	April		S	Soil moist all year
D. catenulata	M	June		S	Soil moist all year

QUICK REFERENCE CHART OF FLOWERING HOUSE PLANTS (Cont.)

SIZE	SUMMER OUTDOORS	EXPOSURE
S (small): to 24 inches	* On porch or in garden	S (sun): 3 to 4 hrs.
M (medium): 24 to 36 inches	for best results	L (bright light): 2 to 3 hrs.
L (large): 36 inches and over		Sh (semishade): 1 to 2 hrs.
V vine		

TIME OF BLOOM: Months Indicated

Plant	Size	Time of Bloom	Summer Outdoors	Exposure	Remarks
Dipladenia amoena	M	June		L	Short rest after flowering
Echeveria Derenbergii	S	Feb		S	Good succulent
Epidendrum stamfordia- num	M	March	*	S	Severe rest after flowering
Epiphyllum oxypetalum	L	July-Aug		S	Awkward grower
Episcia cupreata	V	July-Aug		L	At best in baskets
E. lilacina	V	July-Aug		L	At best in baskets
E. pinkiscia	V	July-Aug		L	At best in baskets
Eranthemum nervosum	S	Nov-March		S	No definite resting time
Eucharis grandiflora	M	April	*	L	Watch for mealy bugs
Eucomis punctata (comosa)	M	July-Aug	*	S	Grows from bulb
Euphorbia pulcherrima	L	Dec-Jan		L	The Christmas Poinsettia
E. splendens	S	Feb-April	*	L	Grow on the dry side
Exacum affine	S	Oct-Dec	*	L	Grow as annual
Fuchsia	M	July-Aug	*	Sh	Difficult, not impossible
Gardenia jasminoides	M	Nov	*	L	Exacting
Gazania rigens	S	April	*	S	Nice foliage too
Gloriosa Rothschildiana	V	July-Aug	*	Sh	Popular tuber plant
Gloxinia (Sinningia)	M	June		L	Keep foliage dry
Guzmania monostachia	M	May	*	L	Keep "vase" filled with water
Haemanthus coccineus	M	Oct		S	Short winter rest
H. Katharinae	M	May		S	Short winter rest
Hedychium coronarium	L	Oct	*	S	Fine patio plant
H. Gardnerianum	L	Sept-Nov	*	S	Fine patio plant
Heliconia angustifolia	L	Oct	*	S	Excellent for patio
H. aurantiaca	L	March-July	*	S	Excellent for patio
H. psittacorum	L	March-April	*	S	Excellent for patio
Hibiscus Rosa-sinensis	L	Nov	*	L	Fine patio plant
Holmskioldia sanguinea	S	Oct		S	Avoid repotting; top-dress
Hoya bella	V	Sept-Oct		Sh	Popular Wax Plant, miniature form
H. carnosa	V	Sept-Oct		Sh	Grow rather dry
H. Keysii	V	Sept-Oct		L	Avoid crowding
H. Motoskei	V	Sept-Oct		L	Grow rather dry

QUICK REFERENCE CHART OF FLOWERING
HOUSE PLANTS (Cont.)

SIZE	SUMMER OUTDOORS	EXPOSURE
S (small): to 24 inches	* On porch or in garden	S (sun): 3 to 4 hrs.
M (medium): 24 to 36 inches	for best results	L (bright light): 2 to 3 hrs.
L (large): 36 inches and over		Sh (semishade): 1 to 2 hrs.
V vine		

TIME OF BLOOM: Months Indicated

Plant	Size	Time of Bloom	Summer Outdoors	Exposure	Remarks
Hydrangea	M	May		S	Gift plant, many kinds
Iboza riparia	M	Dec		S	Nice scent
Impatiens Sultanii	S	July-Aug	*	L	Everblooming in summer
Ixora coccinea	M	March-July	*	L	Starts blooming when young
I. chinensis	M	March-July	*	L	Brilliant red
I. 'Gillette's Yellow'	M	March-July	*	L	Fine yellow
I. javanica	M	March-July	*	L	Another good one
Jacobinia carnea	S	April		L	Always keep moist
J. Ghiesbreghtiana	S	Jan		L	Always keep moist
J. suberecta	S	July		L	Always keep moist
Jatropha pandurifolia	M	July-Sept	*	L	May bloom twice
Kaempferia roscoeana	S	June		L	A flower a day in summer
Kalanchoe Blossfeldiana	M	Dec		S	Grow quite dry
K. Fedtschenkoi	S	Jan		S	Grow quite dry
K. uniflora	S	Jan-March		S	Grow quite dry
K. velutina	S	March-June		S	Grow quite dry
Kohleria amabilis	S	June	*	L	Warmth and humidity
K. bogotensis	M	July	*	L	Warmth and humidity
K. eriantha	M	July	*	L	Warmth and humidity
Lantana montevidensis	V	Feb-April		L	Superior basket plant
Lobularia maritima	S	Dec	*	S	Sweet Alyssum
Lockhartia Oerstedii	M	June-July		L	Keep moist all year
Lycaste aromatica	M	Oct-Nov		Sh	Dry out severely after flowering
Mahernia verticillata	S	March		S	Keep cool
Mammillaria Hahniana	S	Dec	*	S	Good cactus
Mandevilla splendens	V	July-Aug	*	S	Pretty flowers
Manettia bicolor	S	Jan-March		L	Keep pot-bound
Medinilla magnifica	L	Jan	*	L	Only mature plants bloom
Musa nana	L	March	*	Sh	Pot up offshoots
M. velutina	L	March	*	Sh	Dwarf species
Narcissus orientalis	M	Oct-April		L	Yellow flowers
N. Tazetta	M	Oct-April		L	The sweet scented Paper White

QUICK REFERENCE CHART OF FLOWERING HOUSE PLANTS (Cont.)

SIZE	SUMMER OUTDOORS	EXPOSURE
S (small): to 24 inches	* On porch or in garden	S (sun): 3 to 4 hrs.
M (medium): 24 to 36 inches	for best results	L (bright light): 2 to 3 hrs.
L (large): 36 inches and over		Sh (semishade): 1 to 2 hrs.
V vine		

TIME OF BLOOM: Months Indicated

Plant	Size	Time of Bloom	Summer Outdoors	Exposure	Remarks
Neomarica caerulea	M	March	*	L	Keep pot-bound
N. gracilis	M	Jan	*	L	Keep pot-bound
N. Northiana	M	April	*	L	Keep pot-bound
Neoregelia carolinae	L	Oct-Feb	*	Sh	Color for seven months
Nerium Oleander	M	June	*	L	Leaves poisonous
Odontoglossum grande	M	Jan.	*	L	Dry out after flowering
O. pulchellum	S	March		L	Lily-of-the-Valley fragrance
Oncidium ampliatum	M	Feb-March	*	S	Dry out after flowering
O. ornithorynchum	S	Nov-Jan		L	Keep moist all year
Ophthalmophyllum Schlechteri	S	Nov	*	S	Keep dry in winter
Osmanthus fragrans	M	Oct	*	L	Keep pot-bound
Oxalis cernua	S	Feb-May	*	L	Superior flowering plant
O. hirta	S	Jan	*	L	Superior flowering plant
O. melanosticta	S	Sept-Oct	*	L	Superior flowering plant
O. Ortgiesii	S	Everblooming	*	L	Superior flowering plant
O. rosea	S	Everblooming	*	L	Superior flowering plant
Passiflora alato-caerulea	V	April-June	*	L	Difficult at home
P. coccinea	V	May-Aug	*	L	Incredible flowers
Pelargonium	S/M	Various		L	Geranium, fine house plant
Pentas lanceolata	M	Sept-Jan	*	L	Small plants bloom
Petrea volubilis	L	May-Aug		S	Only mature plants bloom
Plumbago capensis	L	July-Aug	*	L	Grow somewhat dry for bloom
Punica Granatum var. nana	S	Oct		L	Good year-round plant
Rechsteineria leucotricha	S	July-Aug		S	Rest after flowering
Reinwardtia indica	S	Feb	*	S	Cool airy condition
Rhipsalis burchelli	M	Jan		S	Humidity and warmth
R. capilliformis	M	Jan		S	Humidity and warmth
R. paradoxa	M	Jan		S	Humidity and warmth
Rivina humilis	S	Sept		S	High humidity
Rosa chinensis var. minima	S	May-Sept	*	S	Cute miniature
Ruellia macrantha	M	Nov-Jan	*	Sh	Bushy
R. Makoyana	S	Nov-Jan	*	Sh	Grow somewhat dry

QUICK REFERENCE CHART OF FLOWERING HOUSE PLANTS (Cont.)

SIZE	SUMMER OUTDOORS	EXPOSURE
S (small): to 24 inches	* On porch or in garden	S (sun): 3 to 4 hrs.
M (medium): 24 to 36 inches	for best results	L (bright light): 2 to 3 hrs.
L (large): 36 inches and over		Sh (semishade): 1 to 2 hrs.
V vine		

TIME OF BLOOM: Months Indicated

Plant	Size	Time of Bloom	Summer Outdoors	Exposure	Remarks
Russelia equisetiformis	M	June	*	L	Dry out somewhat in winter
Schizocentron elegans	V	June		S	Keep somewhat dry
Schizostylis coccinea	M	Sept	*	S	Good house plant
Smithiantha cinnabarina	M	Nov		L	Store tubers when dormant
S. zebrina	L	Aug-Nov		L	Willing bloomer
Solandra guttata	L	Oct	*	S	Big yellow flowers
Solanum Pseudo-Capsicum	S	Dec		S	Temporary house plant
Sparmannia africana	M	Feb		L	Indoor Linden
Sprekelia formosissima	M	April	*	S	Grow crowded
Stephanotis floribunda	V	April	*	L	Give winter rest
Strelitzia Reginae	L	Sept-Oct	*	L	Give poor soil
Streptocarpus Rexii	M	April-July		Sh	Water carefully in winter
Strobilanthes isophyllus	S	March-June	*	L	Make new plants from spring cuttings
Thunbergia alata	V	Dec	*	S	Make new plants from spring cuttings
T. erecta	M	July	*	S	Erect shrub
T. grandiflora	V	Aug-Sept	*	S	Bell-like flowers
Tibouchina semidecandra	S	May-Sept	*	S	Prune and pinch
Tulbaghia fragrans	M	June		L	Agapanthus relative
Vallota speciosa	M	May		S	Grow dry after flowering
Veltheimia viridifolia	L	Dec		S	Grow dry after flowering
Vriesea splendens	S	June-Aug	*	Sh	The Flaming Sword
Zantedeschia aethiopica	M	July-Aug	*	L	White Calla
Z. Elliottiana	M	July-Aug	*	L	Yellow Calla
Z. Rehmannii	M	July-Aug	*	L	Pink Calla
Zephyranthes	M	July-Aug	*	S	Plant 5 bulbs to a 6-inch pot
Zygocactus truncatus (Schlumbergera)	M	Jan-Feb	*	Sh	Dry out in November and give sun
Z. 'Gertrude Beahm'	M	Jan-Feb	*	Sh	Dry out in November and give sun

Selected Bibliography

Ballard, Ernesta Drinker. *Garden in Your House*. New York: Harper & Bros., 1958.

Boutard, C. R. *Plants Indoors*. New York: Abelard-Schuman, Ltd., 1957.

Brilmayer, Bernice. *All About Begonias*. Garden City, N.Y.: Doubleday & Co., Inc., 1960.

Chabot, Ernest. *How to Grow Rare Greenhouse Plants*. New York: M. Barrows & Co., Inc., 1952.

Cherry, Elaine. *Fluorescent Light Gardening*. Princeton, N.J.: D. Van Nostrand Co., Inc., 1965.

Cutak, Ladislaw. *Cactus Guide*. Princeton, N.J.: D. Van Nostrand Co., Inc., 1956.

Flowering Plants from Cuban Gardens. New York: Criterion Books, 1958.

Free, Montague. *All About House Plants*. New York: American Garden Guild & Doubleday & Co., Inc., 1946.

Gannon, Ruth. *Decorating with House Plants*. New York: Studio-Crowell, 1952.

Graf, Alfred Byrd. *Exotica III*. Rutherford, N.J.: Roehrs Company, 1963.

Hersey, Jean, *Woman's Day Book of House Plants*. New York: Simon & Schuster, Inc., 1965.

Kramer, Jack. *Growing Orchids at Your Windows*. Princeton, N.J.: D. Van Nostrand Co., Inc., 1963.

McDonald, Elvin. *Miniature Plants for Home and Greenhouse*. Princeton, N.J.: D. Van Nostrand Co., Inc., 1962.

McDonald, Elvin. *The World Book of House Plants*. Cleveland and New York: World Publishing Co., 1963.

Noble and Merkel. *Plants Indoors*. Princeton, N.J.: D. Van Nostrand Co., Inc., 1954.

Sutcliffe, Alys. *House Plants for City Dwellers*. New York: E. P. Dutton & Co., Inc., 1964.

Wilson, Helen Van Pelt. *The Joy of Geraniums*. New York: M. Barrows & Co., Inc., 1965.

Index

Boldface references are to illustrations

123